Fishing Nantucket

EMENTS

'uley, for all the advice
'blishing process.

A GUIDE FOR ISLAND ANGLERS

CAPTAIN MATT REINEMO

FOR LIZ AND CHICK,
MY INSPIRING WIFE AND SON

TABLE OF CONTENTS

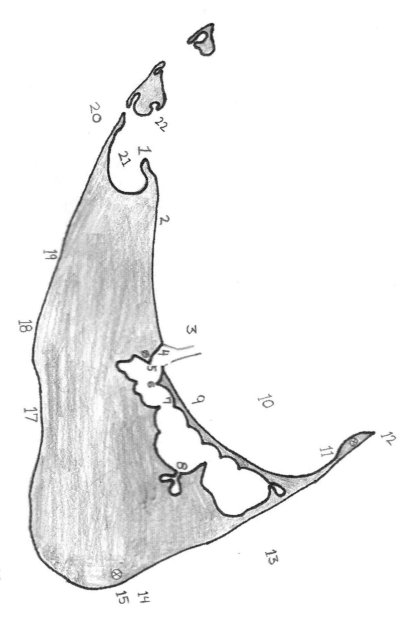

KEY

AN INTRODUCTION
TO FISHING NANTUCKET

The task of writing a "comprehensive" guide to fishing Nantucket is a difficult one. When I first started, the task seemed manageable; after all it is a fairly small island with only a handful of inshore species. Going through the different seasons and different species seemed straightforward, but I started thinking about the different spots, the different lures, and the different tides, each adding another level of complexity. For example, striped bass might as well be a half a dozen totally different species given the methods used and locations in which they are successfully targeted. As I was writing, I would remember an instance here or there where I caught some fish, and my first instinct would be to include it, and discuss how I did it. If I did that, this would quickly devolve into a convoluted tale that could be aptly titled: *All the Fish I have Managed to Catch in My 31 years, and an Imperfect Memory of How it Was Done.*

To avoid that, I needed to decide what information would be necessary and helpful in leading you toward good fishing, and what information was superfluous or misleading and should be omitted. In making that determination, it was necessary to consider you, the reader. I have imagined you to be a person who has done some fishing. Perhaps it has not yet completely taken over your life, but since you are now reading a book about fishing, it is certainly well on its way. For one reason or another, you find yourself wanting to catch some fish on Nantucket. Perhaps you live here, you have started fishing and are looking for a little more success. Maybe you are an experienced angler who will be on Nantucket in August with your family, lying on the beach day-in and day-out will bore you to tears, and you want to know what is biting that time of year and how to go about catching it. Or perhaps you are thinking about a trip to the island specifically for fishing, you want your trip to coincide with good flats fishing for striped bass, and you need a good guide (me!) as well as some advice on how to attempt it on your own. It is my hope that reading this book will address all of those situations.

I travel to fish whenever I am able, and catching some fish in new and different water is absolutely one of my favorite experiences. The first thing I recommend is to call a guide. Being on the water with somebody who is experienced and can take you to the fish and help you catch them is far better than trying to do it from a book. Included is a section on the different boats, captains and options available on Nantucket, because if you are going to fish with a guide, it takes some effort and knowledge to select the right one to fulfill your specific desires.

However, fishing with a guide every day may not be possible, due to budgetary restrictions or other factors, and even if it is possible, it may not be what you want. Catching fish in new water is thrilling, whether you have a guide's help or not, but I am the first to admit that exploring new water on your own, cracking a few of its secrets and catching a few fish relying on only yourself is a great feeling. Fishing with a guide is often a pressure-packed situation. The pressure is on him to find the fish because you are paying him, and the pressure is on you to hold up your end when he does find them, and the clock is ticking on both of you.

I would not call fishing relaxing. When I am fishing I am likely to be about as tightly strung as I get, so relaxing is not the right word. However, the soul-soothing and regenerative powers of fishing, which are undeniable, are often at their best when you are on your own. This book will point you in the right direction, and get you on the water at an appropriate time with the appropriate gear, and hopefully guide you through some of the important details that even experienced fisherman may not be privy to in a new locale. For instance, the mother-of-pearl colored, Magnum Long-A Bomber (known locally and referred to after this as a Pearl Bomber) is a great striper lure and perhaps the most popular one for island anglers. Sankaty is great place to find stripers, perhaps the best spot around the island. But, if you were to go to Sankaty (a great spot) and cast a Pearl Bomber (a great lure), chances are you would not get any stripers, because at Sankaty, the stripers spend most of the time tight to the bottom and your Pearl Bomber will swim within a couple feet of the surface. This book will inform you of these types of small but important details, of the sort that even experienced anglers away from their home waters are not necessarily aware of.

If you are new to fishing, this is a great starting point and it will help you meet with success earlier in your fishing than just striking out on your own with a few brief instructions from a friend or a tackle store clerk. Some of the information may seem too in-depth and there may be some things that escape your understanding, but if you continue fishing, they should quickly become clear. At the very least, this book will keep you from wasting valuable fishing time by nudging you toward productive times, places and techniques.

Finally, for those of you who are already experienced island anglers, perhaps even more so than I, I hope that this book tells you about a new spot, or helps you fine-tune a method with which you are not intimately familiar, or helps you catch a few more fish one way or another. But to be honest, I do not have to sell this book to you at all. You are already hooked on fishing Nantucket's waters, and you will probably greedily read everything written about it, even if you are certain you could do whatever the author is writing about better and more often. Certainly, if the shoe were on the other foot, and you wrote a book about fishing on Nantucket, I would be among the first to run out and buy it.

The thought of writing for this crowd of experienced anglers brings about another question: am I qualified to write this book? I am only thirty-one years old and perhaps a somewhat comprehensive guide to island fishing should be undertaken only by an "Old Salt," who was catching stripers when I was in diapers. Since you are reading this, I have determined for myself that the answer is yes, I am qualified, and to help assuage any concerns you may have, I will give you a brief fishing resume. I was born on Nantucket, and aside from off-season travels to pursue fish and higher education, I have lived here for my entire life. I do not remember the first time I went fishing because it occurred when I was too young to remember anything. In middle school I became a fly fisherman (though not exclusively), at what was probably the beginning of the boom in popularity of saltwater fly-fishing. I became, and still am, an avid reader of fishing periodicals as well as any other fishing literature I get my hands on. While in high school, I worked as a mate for my father and others and I did some beach guiding. When I turned eighteen, I got my captain's license and have run our family's charter boat *Topspin*, out of Straight Wharf ever since. I have also run charter boats in Florida and Costa Rica. In 2001, I started taking clients fishing in smaller boats out of Madaket for stripers on the flats, bonito, and other light-tackle and fly-fishing endeavors. Every year, this becomes a larger part of my business and is some of the best fishing to be had on Nantucket.

When I am not fishing with clients, like most good fishing guides I know, I prefer to spend my time fishing.

For some locations the information is detailed and in-depth, and I am comfortable offering advice garnered through extensive experience (striped bass at Great Point, striped bass on the flats and bonito come to mind), and at the other end of the spectrum, for some of the methods and locations, my knowledge is limited. I would not consider myself an expert on striper fishing with any kind of bait, and I will not be able to fill you in too much on the intricacies of fishing at night because most of my fishing is dawn to dusk. If I am not an expert in a particular area of fishing, I should be able to point you in the right direction and I will try to avoid feeding you any misinformation.

Right now there is a short list of guys in my head who I look up to and regard as great local fisherman. They are uniformly older, more experienced, and perhaps even better qualified to guide you on your island fishing adventures, but there are a couple of problems. First, most of these guys subscribe to the school of thought that while they know how to find and catch the fish, that information is best kept to themselves. They certainly did not tell me how to do it, and now they share information with me only because I have proven myself and often have information and fishing reports they can use to their own advantage. They will probably not attempt to educate the general angling public on their locations and methods.

While I certainly see where they are coming from, and I may kick myself for this project if my favorite spots get crowded and you catch some of "my" fish, I am more of the school of thought that embraces recreational anglers. Once you come to love fishing, hopefully you will come to respect and protect the resources and the environment. Your voice as a recreational angler may be heard in politics, helping shape more responsible and conservation-minded fisheries management that prioritizes the recreational angler. Hopefully, by telling you how to catch some fish I may have saved for myself, it will eventually make the fishing better for both of us, and more importantly, for our children.

Most of the guys on my short list are almost exclusively big boat guys, deep-water stripers and bluefin tuna being their forte. They came of age before fly rods and flats arrived in the culture of striper fishing, and for whatever reason, perhaps their considerable success elsewhere, they didn't take it up. They would be able to advise you on flats fishing about as well as I can advise you on how to catch stripers with live scup. Being that they know guys who do it, they know where it is done, and given their general knowledge of angling they would probably be pretty good at it if they put in some time, but that is about it. Likewise, the best of the flats and bonito crowd would probably not be able to give you the wire-line specifics. I consider myself to be a well-rounded island angler. I am a fly fisherman and light-tackle enthusiast when I fish for fun and when I have clients who are the same, while at the same time, I have spent the last thirteen seasons running a big boat chasing stripers and blues mostly in big water.

The last reason to let me guide you in your saltwater pursuits, and perhaps the only important one, is that I sat down and wrote the book. Local knowledge is critical, especially when inshore fishing and there is no other literature that will guide you in the specifics of fishing Nantucket.

I have organized the book first by species and then by season. For striped bass and bluefish, I will take you from their arrival in late April or May through their departure around October or November, touching on locations and methods that are effective during the different seasons. I will also cover bonito, false albacore, and a variety of bottom species, but without seasonal analysis largely because they are short-term visitors, or (in the case of bottom species) the methods and spots do not change much with the season.

The lines marking seasons, and even species, are never as clear as the demarcations in the book, and that should constantly be kept in mind. It is my intent that the species and then seasonal organization itself will be the first step toward better fishing. It will help you avoid such mistakes as planning a trip to Nantucket to fish for stripers on the flats in early August, or even worse, deciding to try for a few bonito on beautiful day in June.

Nantucket is also a fine jumping off point for some very good offshore action, which I will touch upon, but only to point you in the right direction. I love offshore fishing, and I do it whenever I am able. I have done it with success, and I have done it around the world, but I have not done it often enough to write an in depth how-to book on it (yet). There have been many great books and magazine articles about offshore fishing that are applicable to the world-class offshore fishing we have off Nantucket. While local knowledge never hurts, it is far less critical in the world of offshore fishing than inshore fishing. No matter where you fish offshore, many of the same tactics are applicable in the waters off Nantucket. While I was able to answer the question "Am I qualified to write this book?" in the affirmative for myself in regards to inshore fishing, I am not qualified to give you bluefin tuna fishing advice over Bobby DeCosta and Pete Kaizer or advise you on how to catch white marlin as well as Josh Eldridge or Doug Lindley.

Keep in mind that while it is my intent to give you a broad and inclusive picture of saltwater fishing around Nantucket, to write an all-inclusive guide is impossible. There are many more methods, spots and lures out there, and my failure to touch upon them within these pages should not deter you from trying them.

I hope you enjoy the book, and I hope it helps you catch more fish. Whether more means going from zero to one, from bluefish to stripers, from stripers to bonito, or from too many fish to count to slightly more than too many fish to count, I believe it can help.

CHAPTER ONE

Striped Bass

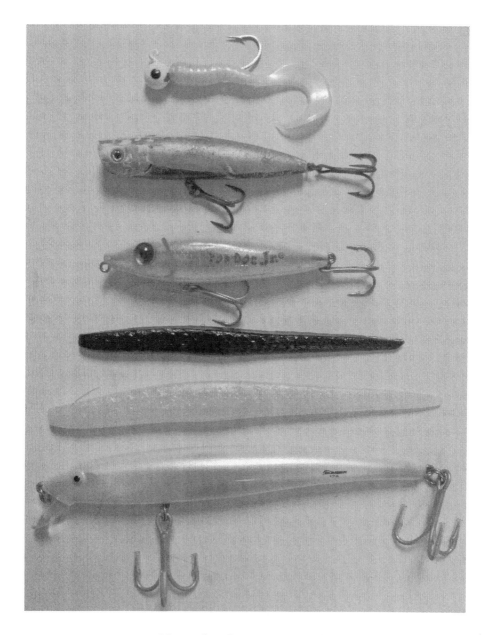

Nantucket Striper Essentials

Top to Bottom: Spofford's Joppa Jog, A well used popper on its 2nd or 3rd paint job, Mirrolure for "Walking the Dog," 6" Skinny Hogy, 7" Original Hogy, Pearl Bomber

I am not old enough to remember when Striped Bass fishing was good, before it was bad. Throughout my childhood in the 1980s and early 90s, striped bass were somewhat mythical and totally out of my league. They were pursued only by the most dogged, knowledgeable anglers, usually at bizarre times. Even in the rare event you caught one it would most likely have to be released because the keeper-size was a massive thirty-six inches. Bluefish were the predominant quarry amongst all but the cagiest anglers. The bumper sticker "Think Bluefish" was very popular, as if thinking about striped bass was either depressing or arrogant. Then, in perhaps the greatest conservation success story in history, populations rebounded, striped bass began to reappear in the minds of most anglers, and shortly thereafter, they began to catch them again. I have not seen a "Think Bluefish" bumper sticker in quite some time, and most anglers are now busy thinking stripers.

I have fished for as long as I can remember, drowning worms in the local ponds with my mother and chasing bluefish with my father and brother. In the mid-nineties, saltwater fly fishing was experiencing a boom in popularity, my own fishing was becoming more than a hobby on its way to taking over my life, and striped bass populations were rising. I had many years of fishing under my belt before I ever caught a striper, and for a while they continued to elude me even as those anglers around me (older, more experienced, luckier) began to encounter them from time to time. I do not recall the year, but I finally caught my first striper on a trolled swimming plug (I can still picture it to this day, though I cannot imagine an instance in which I would tie it on again), next to the 5-can buoy off of the East Jetty. The next spring, I enjoyed my first consistent success off the south shore beaches in the early spring, which is, at least to some degree, why I still have a soft spot for returning to these beaches in early May for the chance to tangle with a couple of schoolies. The following year, I caught my first keeper. I was on the ocean side of Coatue in the middle of the day looking for bluefish with a fly rod and popper, and a pod of stripers started busting on some bait right in front of me. It was a fish caught almost entirely by luck, being in the wrong place at the right time and managing not to step on my fly line.

Rather than quench my thirst, each taste of striped bass success only made me eager for more. It has been exciting and wonderful to acquaint myself with stripers just as anglers along the entire east coast have gotten reacquainted with them.

Once they were plentiful again, striped bass quickly claimed the top spot in the hearts and minds of east coast anglers, and it did not really matter whether they had been temporarily displaced, discovered for the first time, or perhaps in quite a few cases, had never left. Nantucket is no exception and the striper is the island's premier inshore gamefish.

It is hard to say what makes a species more glamorous and more sought after than another fish, but it is probably a combination of factors. As far as fighting ability goes, the bluefish certainly stacks up admirably against the striped bass. Generally speaking, bluefish do not make the long runs of a striper, but they make up for it with enthusiastic acrobatics and a never-say-die attitude.

As table fare most people prefer the mild, white flaky flesh of the striped bass to bluefish, but that could hardly be the reason the striped bass has assumed a more glamorous position in angler's hearts and minds. Catch and release is the norm for most of the world's glamorous gamefish, such as bonefish, tarpon, permit and billfish. The duration of the stripers' stay could play a role; they arrive in the spring and stay until fall, and even during the height of summer they are targeted quite successfully. Bonito and false albacore are an absolute blast, and they have their devout followers, but compared to stripers they are short-term guests in Nantucket's waters.

Size is surely a factor. Stripers are the largest of the inshore gamefish found in the Northeast. Fish of twenty pounds are fairly common, thirty pounders are certainly around and fish anywhere from forty to the recent world record of eighty-two pounds are within the realm of possibility.

In the end, difficulty may be what gives striped bass the top spot. It is largely true that catching a bluefish is easier than catching a striped bass. There are days that striped bass will be fighting over your lure, jumping all over themselves in order to be hooked, as well as days when you could look all over Nantucket Sound to find one bluefish, and when you do find him, he won't bite. However, for the most part, it is more difficult to catch a striped bass than a bluefish. Gamefish that are looked upon as difficult to catch are generally more sought after than easy ones. Take for example jack crevalle and permit; both are silver, platter-shaped fish, similar in size, fast and fun to catch, but the later is the top prize of tropical flats and the former is largely regarded as something to pull on if nothing else is biting. As a general rule in angling, doing things in a difficult manner makes them more satisfying; catching a fish on fly is better than catching it on a lure, catching fish on 8lbs. test is preferable to the same fish on 20lbs. test, and going out and catching fish on a rod and reel is preferable to just going to the fish market.

Most likely it is combination of all these factors, and perhaps many more, varying from angler to angler, that gives the striped bass top billing. I would say the top spot is well deserved. Fishing for striped bass presents you with many different options in terms of tactics and locations. No other fish is found in as many different types of areas and successfully targeted in as many different ways as the striped bass. You can successfully fish for stripers at midnight, with live bait, in water forty feet deep just as you can fish for them at noon, with lures, in water two feet deep. You will find them tucked deep within creeks and estuaries, and occasionally one will bite a tuna lure thirty miles offshore. Determining when, where, how and with what to start off with can be very difficult given all the viable options available to you. Having a lot of options to choose from is a good problem to have, and perhaps is another reason why the striped bass is king of the inshore gamefish.

THE FIRST ARRIVALS

I have always enjoyed heading out in the early spring and over the years I have dedicated a lot of time and energy to fish and fishing that a few months later would scarcely cause me to raise an eyebrow. Stripers arrive in Nantucket's waters in late April or early May. The first fish to arrive are schoolies, ranging in size from about ten inches to the mid-twenties. Typically, the first fish of the year arrive along the south shore. It can be pretty chilly in late April and early May, especially standing on a south shore beach. By the time the fish arrive though, it has been a pretty long winter, and if you do choose to head out in search of the first arrivals of the spring, you probably will run into a few other people who are tired of oiling reels, tying flies, and reading about fishing rather than doing it.

The best way to anticipate when the first stripers will arrive is to get fishing reports from Martha's Vineyard. That is certainly not as romantic or perhaps not as satisfying as some kind of old-time outdoors wisdom, something along the lines of "the first stripers of the season will arrive when the south exposed daffodils bloom and the ospreys have nested," but infinitely more effective. Once they have caught stripers on the Vineyard, there will probably be some around Nantucket as soon as the next day, and certainly within the week.

While it does not take much to get Northeast anglers excited in early spring, the early stripers are not without virtue. As their nickname implies, schoolies are generally not alone. Once you have located them, catching several is the norm. Additionally, they are usually hungry, not terribly picky about lures or flies, and you can catch them on your schedule. It is not necessary to fish at sunset or sunrise, or any particular tide. The fish will usually be cruising up and down the shore all day, and fishing at noon can be just as productive as sunset.

Pond openings, if available, are one of the best places to start. The town of Nantucket usually opens Sesachacha Pond and Hummock Pond at some point during the spring by digging a trench through the beach that separates those ponds from the ocean, in order to allow river herring to enter the ponds to spawn. Striped bass often congregate around these openings attracted by the warm water and abundant food supply including herring. Some of the stripers are probably holdovers that have lived in the pond since the last opening or longer, but if there are stripers around the island when the pond is opened, they will be lured toward the opening as well.

If no pond is open, fishing anywhere along the South Shore can be productive. Miacomet is a personal favorite of mine, probably due to its proximity to my house. I have had some great days with schoolies at Tom Never's and Madaket beaches as well. A couple seasons ago in early May, I had practice at the Tom Never's field for a men's baseball league. I brought a couple rods along, and after practice I went to my car and exchanged my glove and cleats for some waders and went down to the beach. Three of my teammates were also fishermen, and though none of them had brought waders or tackle, they followed me down to the water. Breakers surrounded a nice little basin of deep water adjacent to the beach, and my Joppa Jig was eaten on the first cast. There were plenty of stripers in the little basin, and more cruising the shore. My teammates lack of waders was a non-issue as the fish were tight to the shore, and there was enough action for all of us. The four of us traded the two rods back and forth and enjoyed constant action for a little over an hour, until the sun went down and we headed home. It was the perfect early spring, low pressure, outing that comes from just remembering to put your rods in the car.

While the stripers are generally not picky, there are certainly some go-to lures in the early spring. Plastics on jig heads are the standard. Spofford's Joppa Jig is a local favorite, but any jig head with a plastic tail is a good bet. White or red are my favorite colors for the jig head, and I have always had the most success with white plastics. A slow, sporadic retrieve is the most effective method for these lures, letting the jig sink all the way to the bottom and bounce into the sand before giving it another crank or two and making it bounce again. These jigs are especially effective because they are largely immune to wave action, and continue to bounce along down at the bottom of the ocean.

Poppers are also a very good choice for the early arrivals. I especially like to fish poppers when the wind is at my back, flattening out, to some degree, the surf on Nantucket's South Shore. Fishing a popper in the heavy surf is difficult, because the lure often gets caught in the breaking waves where it is impossible to impart any action and it often gets tangled. On choppy days, I revert back to the plastic on a jig head.

When retrieving poppers, give your rod a sharp pull, causing the lure to chug under the surface and throw up a wall of water. Often, it helps to keep your rod low, which causes the lure to get pulled under the water, creating a gurgling sound and a large bubbling wave. If you pull with your rod tip up, the lure will often skip along the surface of water, creating some splashing and noise on the surface, but not causing the loud underwater noise and disturbance you want in order to attract the fish. Also keep in mind that if your lure is splashing along the surface, it is much more likely to get tangled in it's own treble hooks than if it is chugging through the water.

Once you have pulled your rod, reel in the slack you have created with the pull in preparation for the next chug, but do not be in any hurry to do it again. While you are gathering the slack, the popper is floating back to surface, and hopefully being inspected by an eager striper. Often times the fish will hit the lure while it is sitting totally motionless on the surface. Experiment with different types of retrieves until you find what the fish prefer, which may change from outing to outing. Sometimes you will have the most luck giving your lure another chug immediately after it returns to the surface, and other times letting it sit motionless for several seconds will draw more strikes.

Fishing poppers, or topwaters, in the early spring has many advantages. Some days you will find that you are getting more strikes than someone else on the beach fishing with a jig. If you have already caught a few fish on a jig, and are looking for some larger fish, perhaps even one of the first keepers of the season, a topwater plug is a good choice to try and draw the attention of the largest fish in the area. When fishing topwater at any time, but especially during the early spring when the fish tend to be small, be prepared to miss more strikes than you would when using subsurface lures. Once a striper decides to eat a topwater lure, they usually commit whole-heartedly. They will smack the lure with ferocity. Upon seeing such a strike, the angler's first instinct is to quickly set the hook. While this will sometimes result in hooking the fish, often it will result in pulling the lure out of its mouth, or pulling a lure that was not in the fish's mouth further away from it. The striper's first attack on the lure is often so enthusiastic, that the lure is actually knocked away from its mouth, either by the fish itself or the wall of water created by the fish coming at the lure from below. Either way, you don't want to move the lure any further away from the fish. It is extremely difficult to remain disciplined at this point because the strike is visible, and often audible as well, leaving most anxious anglers intent on prematurely setting the hook, but you need to hold off setting the hook until you feel the fish, rather than just see it. Once the striper does have the lure in its mouth, you will have enough time to set the hook once you feel it. If the lure is not in the fish's mouth after the first strike, they will often take another crack it. If I get a strike and I don't hook the fish, I like to let the lure sit still for a few seconds, then barely twitch it for a few seconds, before continuing my retrieve. While I don't have a foundation of biological evidence to support this theory, I imagine this to be how a baitfish that was just attacked by a striper might behave: the baitfish might first experience a brief period of total immobility or unconsciousness after the failed attack, followed by a gradual awakening. While I do not know if my method actually mimics bait, I do know that it often produces repeat strikes, which is all that really counts.

Nonetheless, even if your angling is perfect, you are going to have some strikes that do not result in hooking a fish. Maybe the fish got enough of the lure on the first swipe to think twice about hitting it again, maybe they just lost interest, or maybe they caught a glimpse of more bait; in any case, sometimes a fish that misses the lure the first time just does not come back. This can be especially aggravating after a long fishless winter, but since we are talking about fishing amidst schoolies, there is the strong possibility of another chance at a striper in short order. And while a missed strike may result in a fishless trip, it is just as effective as landing a fish in terms of announcing the end of winter and the return of stripers, which is at least part of the goal in an early season trip, and an excellent reason to go back again tomorrow.

When fishing along the south shore for the earliest striped bass of the season, I fish with jig heads and plastics or poppers almost exclusively, but other offerings can certainly be effective. Scaled down versions swimming plugs or crank baits, such as the Pearl Bomber (which becomes a striper staple later in the season), are sometimes worthwhile options, but I tend to stay away from them because they are often rigged with two or more treble hooks, and these seem to find their way into a striper's throat much more often than those on a popper. Small spoons such as Deadly Dicks or Hopkins and lifelike plastics such as Storm Minnows can also be effective.

For fly fishermen, Nantucket's South Shore can be a difficult and frustrating place. Large surf makes stripping baskets a necessity, and the wave action can wreak havoc with your line on the water. My fly rod usually stays at home for the first couple days or weeks until the fish move into Nantucket Harbor, presenting themselves beautifully in situations tailor made for fly fishing. Additionally, on those first few trips out in the spring, after coming off a few fishless months, actually catching fish seems more important than it will become in a few short weeks, and a fly rod is seldom the most effective tool if just catching fish is one's main priority.

For those dedicated to fly fishing, catching these early arrivals is certainly possible. An intermediate sinking line will alleviate some of difficulty caused by the wave action. Streamers, such as Deceivers and Clousers retrieved at a slow, steady rate are the best bet. Bouncing a weighted fly off the bottom, similar to fishing a jig head and plastic can also be very effective.

The fish, and thus the lures, are small at this point, and light tackle is definitely what is called for. Six to twelve pound outfits are perfect; they allow for adequate touch and feel with the light lures, and they don't completely overpower the little stripers. Many locals don't break out their heavier traditional saltwater surfcasting gear for a few more weeks; they hit the beaches early in the year with their freshwater tackle instead.

Once the stripers arrive on the South Shore, it will not be long until they are everywhere. Nantucket Harbor and the eastern shore of the island, from Sankaty all the way to Great Point, are likely places to find stripers. Allowing for exceptions based on weather, wind direction, pond openings and trustworthy reports or suspect rumors of good fishing, my usual springtime routine begins with the South Shore and Great Point for the first arrivals, followed by early spring fishing in Nantucket Harbor, and culminates on the flats of Madaket for as long as the fish are present.

After my first successful trip of the season, for which the purpose is merely to bend a rod and catch any sized striper after their long winter absence, my focus usually becomes catching the island's first keeper (as of this writing the legal keeper size is 28" from its nose to a squeezed tail), and failing that, my own personal first keeper. By June, I am a pretty standard catch-and-release angler, though my first few keepers of the year usually end up on the dinner table. In either case, the tackle and tactics stay the same. Generally, the first keeper is barely over 28" and the best way to catch it is to find some schoolies in the mid-twenty inch range and keep fishing them hoping for the biggest of the bunch. Sometimes keepers arrive only a few days after the first fish of the year, and sometimes a couple weeks later.

At some point in the early spring, I usually take a ride to Great Point. Usually, the Great Point trips are taken for the purpose of catching the first keeper, and I have been lucky enough to find it there a couple times, but it is just as likely that the wind is out of the southwest and I don't feel like fishing with a cold wind in my face. One of the overlooked beauties of fishing Nantucket is that you can always fish in the lee (out of the wind) by using the island to block the wind. Of course, the wind in your face may blow the bait and fish in tight to the shore, and if you're the type of fisherman who is going fishing in Nantucket in early spring at all, you probably don't mind a little wind, but if you're as likely as not to find fish in the lee, why not fish there?

On the early spring trips to Great Point, I have always had the most luck on the eastern, ocean facing side, anywhere from a hundred yards to a mile south of the lighthouse and the rip. I use exactly the same tackle and tactics as when I am fishing the South Shore, usually a white plastic on a jig head bounced slowly along the bottom. For fly fishermen, a stripping basket is still recommended, and there is still some wave action but fishing along the eastern shore is much easier than battling the surf on the south side.

Another advantage to fishing the eastern shore is that it is possible to see the fish, an impossibility in the South Shore surf. Oftentimes schools of fish will be cruising the eastern shore just beyond the first drop off, only five or ten feet from where you are standing. In the clear water of spring, the fish as well as their shadows on the bottom are sometimes visible. When you are fishing here, keep an eye out for them and try to put a cast in front of them if you see them. Usually they will be swimming back and forth along the shore, and it can be more productive to stay in a spot they seem to be frequenting rather than trying to stay with them. If you do put a cast in front of a few fish and you don't get a bite, consider a lure change.

Although it is difficult, it is sometimes possible to see them from your car on the drive out. If you are in the passenger seat, I recommend keeping your eyes on the water right where it is clear enough to see, just beyond the waves. I wouldn't recommend ever just doing a drive-by because most of the time the fish will not be visible from the car, but occasionally you can luck into a school of fish you would've passed by.

SPRINGTIME STRIPERS

Striper fishing is at its absolute best in the spring. Often you hear about fall fishing, encountering the stripers as they head south, gorging themselves along the way. Unfortunately, at least in recent years, striper fishing in the fall has paled in comparison to the spring. It seems to me that while the fish may pass through in the fall and eat along the way, they are still just passing through. Whereas in the spring the stripers seem to arrive hungry and set up shop in Nantucket's waters. You may have fantastic, world class action in September and October, but you may also get blanked; in June the question is not so much if will you find fish, but rather how many.

Striper fishing is firing on all cylinders by mid-June. The fish are everywhere from the South Shore, to the flats, to Sankaty and the Eastern rips. With the possible exception of fishing off Great Point's edge for stripers (which for the last couple years has heated up late in June and stayed good through mid-July) just about every method and location discussed in these pages should be good in the spring.

If you are considering a fishing trip to Nantucket, and stripers are your species of choice, June should be your first choice.

Nantucket Harbor

For small boat and shore-bound anglers, as well as those who just love to fish in relatively tranquil waters, Nantucket Harbor offers excellent striped bass fishing. Fishing in Nantucket Harbor heats up pretty quickly. When the fish arrive, water temperatures around the island are still at the very bottom of striped bass' comfort range and the harbor holds the warmest water around. While my earliest trips are usually to the South Shore and Great Point, the harbor is the first place I expect fairly consistent fishing.

Nantucket Harbor is very large, extending from Nantucket's downtown, Brant Point, and the Boat Basin, northeast about six miles to Coskata and Wauwinet. Within the harbor there are holes and channels with depths of twenty or more feet, like those off Second Point and Brant Point, as well as expansive flats averaging only a few feet of water. There are sandbars creating rips off Pocomo and Second Point, along with a variety of structure in the form of docks, moorings, and some of the rockiest shorelines the island has to offer, not to mention a number of creeks and inlets trickling in from surrounding estuaries. Given all this diversity around the harbor, there is any number of ways to catch a striper within the harbor itself: fly fishing the flats in bends of Coatue; wire-lining the deep holes off Second Point, First Point, and the east jetty; live-lining an eel off Brant Point; or casting a plug along Hulbert Avenue and the west jetty.

In the interest of starting somewhere, I will start with my favorite place to fish in Nantucket Harbor. While thinking about writing this guide, this is one of two spots I considered leaving out and keeping to myself. Not because it is a totally secret spot where I am the only one to have ever fished, and not because the fishing there is far and away better than any other similar spot, but merely because I have had pretty consistent fishing there for quite a few years and I have never run into anyone else while fishing there. Under these circumstances, it is easy to think of a spot as your own, and I have come to regard this little place as my spot. While I did not hesitate to divulge what I know about Great Point, Sankaty and other well-known island hot spots, the thought of sharing "my spot" made me think twice. But, as is now obvious, I have decided to include it. Maybe it has something to do the fact that the spot isn't really much of a secret at all, or perhaps because there is room for a handful of anglers to fish simultaneously, or because when fishing Nantucket Harbor in May and June, when this spot is at its best, crowds are not really much of a concern. In fact, running into a fellow angler or two might be nice if only to swap reports and bear witness to each other's success. As for the other spot I considered leaving out, it is only big enough for one and you are on your own (I am no saint).

In any case, after the early season runs to the South Shore and Great Point, and before flats fishing in Madaket heats up, you will probably find me at "my spot" on the southern end of Pocomo Head, just north of where Polpis harbor empties into Nantucket Harbor at the mouth of Medouie Creek. Right where the creek flows out, the bottom is sandy and shallow. Once you wade out, the bottom turns grassy, and that is where I start fishing. If you wade straight west, toward town, you can't go very far before the water will be up over your waders, but if you cast toward town you should find some fish. I was content with this spot and I think it was a couple of seasons before I headed south and west onto the flats, because it seemed that there were always a few fish there ready to pounce on a topwater offering. On all but the windiest days, the harbor is perfect for fishing topwater. The retrieves and tactics for poppers described earlier in the first arrivals section remain the same.

A topwater offering that I am partial to, especially in the harbor and on the flats, is a walk-the-dog type lure, such as Zara Spooks, the Mirro-Lure Dog series, or the Bomber Badonk-A-Donk. To retrieve these lures, give your rod-tip a slight twitch toward you, then reel in the slack, and then twitch it again. If done correctly, the lure will zigzag back and forth across the surface moving left to right as much as back toward you, and that action is called "walking the dog". It is easy to get the hang of with some practice, and it is possible to vary the speed of your retrieve a great deal. You can make it zigzag quickly back and forth or have it scoot left, pause, then scoot back right. Walk-the-dog type lures are more often associated with other species, such as redfish, tarpon, snook and freshwater bass, but they definitely belong in your striper arsenal. Their action certainly excites and attracts fish, and the bites they induce are startling.

The surface commotion made by walking the dog is somewhat subtle, which is why I prefer to use them in the harbor and on the flats. If there is some chop on the water, the action of walk-the-dogs can easily be disrupted and obscured. If that is the case, you may want to go with a floating, chugger-type popper, such as a Smack-it.

In addition to fishing straight out and back toward town, you can wade south toward the Polpis Harbor channel and head to the southeast where there is a large flat. I like to fish this flat with Hogys (versatile soft plastics) or flies, in the same manner I will discuss in the section devoted to flats fishing. There are several little sandy holes on this flat, and stripers often lay in the holes. Also, moving fish often parallel the shore, swimming right along the line where it goes from sand to grass and the depth drops off by about a foot. The entire flat can be productive, and you can wade nearly to the Polpis Harbor channel, though be careful once you approach the channel because it drops off quickly.

This spot offers two of the best harbor fishing terrains where you can utilize the corresponding methods. You can cast a topwater, suspending, or swimming plug in depths of six to ten feet, or even fish live bait there, or you can venture into the shallows with Hogys or walk-the-dog lures. The entire area fishes best on the outgoing tide, when the warmer water, and ostensibly bait, is coming out of Polpis Harbor and the surrounding creeks. Most tide charts will give the time of the tide at Brant Point, and the tide at this particular spot is about an hour and a half later. Arriving two or three hours after the high tide listed for town will give you plenty of time with good conditions. Certainly, if the outgoing tide corresponds with dawn or dusk, that improves your odds even further.

The West Jetty

Back when saltwater fly fishing was really starting to take off in the 1990s, if there was a falling tide in the evening or in the early morning, you could count on a line of fly fishermen, sometimes a dozen or more, standing in waist deep water and casting out, starting at the west jetty and extending back toward Brant Point. The sandbar there enabled them to wade pretty far offshore, perhaps fifty yards or more depending on the tide. Fly fishing was the hip thing to do and the sandbar on the harbor side of the west jetty was the hip spot. It seemed to be the starting point for most of the fly fishing and all the fly-fishing conversations. Around that time I never remember seeing any spin fisherman there, for what reason I do not know, other than it would have been difficult for them to get a good spot amid all the fly anglers.

After a few years of this craze, the sandbar off the west jetty returned to being just another spot. There are still plenty of times when you will find a fisherman there, but now they are probably just as likely to be a plug caster or a bait fisherman, and it is not likely that you will have to fight a crowd to fish it.

The area earned a top spot in my early list of places to fish for stripers in a backward sort of way, because in retrospect it should not have rendered as much success as it did. Early in my fly-fishing career, after my freshman year of high school, I was anchored off the sandbar, a little offshore, in a small Boston Whaler. It was August, and my fishing buddy was a fellow teen equally enthusiastic about fly fishing. We were drawn there not by striped bass, but by the bonito that were busting here and there around the area that day. We were getting some decent shots at them, but we had not gotten any bites, when a few bonito popped up within an easy cast's range. I laid my Epoxy Minnow (the hot fly at the time, which much like the spot, has gone from en vogue to just another fly in the box) into the fray, and retrieved it with high hopes. I failed to get a bite, and threw the minnow back out, but the busts were less feverish and it seemed the bulk of the bonito were moving on. Despite my fading hope, after a couple strips my line came tight, and after a short run, it felt as if I had a cinder block on the end of my line. The fish was intent on remaining right where it was, and I was intent on moving it. Today, even if I did not recognize that fighting style as a striper's right away I would immediately rule out the speedy and frantic bonito. However, at the time I was short on striper, not to mention bonito, experience and I made the logical assumption that since I cast into a school of jumping bonito, that was what had eaten my Epoxy Minnow.

After a tug of war, which seemed positively epic at the time, but no doubt lasted less than a couple minutes, my companion and I were surprised to see a striper beside the boat. At the time, it was the largest striper I had ever caught, but before we could measure it, my companion grabbed the leader and the fish liberated itself with a splash of the tail, an impetuous decision on his part that did not please me. I would guess that the fish was in the thirty-inch range, but given my lack of experience and the passage of time, I could be way off. This was before I knew about the accepted, and often face-saving, system whereby a fish is considered caught when the leader is touched, and at the time, the leader snapping seemed a tragedy. I wanted to hold that fish, take the obligatory photos of it, measure it and hope it exceeded the keeper limit, (which at the time was 32"), but most importantly just savor my victory a little longer and more tangibly. While I like the leader-touching definition of a "caught fish," and certainly the fish are better off the less they are handled, I will admit it can be a little anticlimactic, especially if the fish is some kind of first or in any way remarkable, and particularly if the fish's liberation comes after the leader touching but still before you affect its release.

In any case, this retroactively "caught" striper led to a confidence in me the way that seeing fly fisherman stacked along the beach did not, as I think can often be the case. No matter how many good reports we hear about a certain method or a certain spot, they just do not inspire confidence like a little taste of our own success. From then on I had conviction that there were in fact stripers off the West Jetty, despite the fact I would be fishing for them primarily in the spring rather than the height of August, and at differing tides. I do not think I disregarded these highly important factors, so much I as I just didn't have the answers to the questions they posed. Not having a better place to look, the logical spot to start looking for them was where I found one last summer. The droves of fly fisherman didn't hurt either.

In any case, I started fishing the area regularly, usually on the falling tide, and it usually fished better earlier in the tide rather than later. A spinning rod was my usual choice, having determined them a more effective tool to target the stripers with, and having not caught enough stripers to want to handicap myself. On one memorable evening, I had waded out to the sandbar and was throwing a chugger-type popper out toward the channel. I had not been fishing long when a nice striper enthusiastically attacked the plug. I brought him in and was trying to get a hand on him in the belly button deep water when he made a dive and seemed to try and swim between my legs. He did not make it because one of the treble hooks found its way through my waders and into my thigh. After a brief but painful struggle with one hook in the fish's mouth and the other in my thigh, I managed to unhook the fish, which probably was destined for dinner anyway but it certainly sealed the deal when it hooked me. I waded back to my car, dropped the fish at home, and made my way to the emergency room at Nantucket Cottage Hospital. Physician Assistant Alan Chaffee was on duty and he understood the importance of saving my waders, but he couldn't help himself when it came to needling me a little bit, that I, with my aspirations of fishing proficiency and distinction, was the first of what always promised to be many fishhook removals for him throughout the summer. When he doubted my version of events, I made him call my mother to confirm that there was a large striped bass in my garage that was indeed responsible for the injury at hand.

Eventually, I found success at other spots, and the harbor side of the West Jetty became just another spot on my list rather than the consistent headliner, just as it had with fly fishermen shortly before. It is still a great spot, and these days you are not likely to encounter a crowd. I always had the most success there on topwater plugs (but that is at least in part due to the fact that I was using them most of the time). The water drops off enough (down to five feet or more) beyond the sandbar that a swimming plug can be fished effectively. Suspending twitch baits such as mirrolures and subsurface plastics, such as Storm Minnows or Hogys rigged with some weight, are also an excellent option. If you are wading, you will be confined to the sandbar, which is a large area, extending from against the jetties along the shore in front of Hulbert Avenue, all the way to Brant Point. It can all be productive water, but once you get a few hundred yards south of the jetties, you will need to contend with moorings and the boats on them. If you are in a boat, you can extend your fishing out away from shore. I have found the most productive water to be within a cast length or two from the rocks out to the low spot in the jetty, about halfway out, where the water washes over it at high tide.

The harbor is also a popular and productive spot for live-eel fishing, and this spot is no exception. I have known people to have success by drifting an unweighted eel behind their boat as the tide carries them out, or beach fisherman casting the eels and retrieving them very slowly. Conventional wisdom calls for a drop back, which means giving a slack line once a striper eats a live eel to let the fish maneuver the eel into its mouth and swallow it without feeling any tension from the angler. That is easily accomplished if you are drifting the eel behind your boat with your bail flipped and the line through your finger. When you get a bite, you let the line slip off your finger and the slack is accomplished (when using a conventional reel, leave the drag on free-spool and put your thumb on the spool until there is a bite). Effectuating a drop back becomes a much more difficult task if you are casting an eel from the shore, because the drag on your reel needs to be engaged in order to retrieve the eel. In my recent reading, anglers are finding success in casting eels and using almost no drop back, never free spooling the reel and giving the fish only what slack can be accomplished by dropping the rod tip toward the fish once they feel a bite. In his book, *The Surfcaster's Guide to the Striper Coast*, D.J. Muller advocates a slow retrieve, keeping a little tension on your eel to feel its movements and keep him from burrowing or tangling himself in the leader. Once a bite is felt, dropping your tip and taking three steps toward to the fish will provide an effective drop back.

On more than one occasion I have fished the west jetty and happily caught some fish on topwater lures, only to see a nearby angler with eels pull out a much bigger fish. If you are inclined toward eel fishing, especially in shallow water, this is a spot that should not be overlooked.

Deep Water in the Harbor

The harbor is also home to fine deep-water fishing, both trolling wire line or eels on weighted rigs. If you take just a few steps off Brant Point to the east, you will quickly find yourself in about forty feet of water. Just south of First Point there is a deep channel that drops to more than twenty feet, shallows up to around ten feet in spots as it moves east through first bend, and drops back down to more than twenty feet in a large hole off Second Point. The water just west of the east jetty from the rock pile at the entrance to the 5 Can is about twenty feet. Striped bass are often found in these deep holes, especially in the springtime, but fall can be excellent as well and sometimes even the height of summer can be productive. Wire lining, tackle and methods are discussed at length in the Sankaty section and it is largely similar in these locations. One difference is that shortening your wire from 150 feet to 120 or even one hundred will help keep you off the bottom, but unless you plan to fish that rod exclusively in the harbor, I would not recommend rigging a wire-line setup with less than 150 feet of wire. Dropping out an inch or two of backing rather that the ten to thirty feet recommended for Sankaty, and then trolling a little faster will also help keep you off the bottom. A drawback to wire-lining the harbor is that is can be very labor intensive. As opposed to Sankaty, where you have miles of deep, open, productive water to troll around, these holes in the harbor are comparatively tiny. They are too small to troll around in circles, which means you must drop your lines out, timing the descent of your lures to coincide with the drop-off in depth, fish the stretch of productive water, then reel in, check you lines, swing your boat around, and drop them back out again. As is the case at Sankaty and elsewhere, you will have more success trolling with the tide, rather than against it. Oftentimes the harbor is weedy, your jig will get covered up with weeds quickly if it hits the bottom and sometimes even when it doesn't hit the bottom. While trolling these spots is certainly productive, and you definitely have a shot at some big fish, it often takes a little precision and a lot of cranking.

These deep water holes are also often fished with live bait, and I would say Brant Point, and the forty-plus foot channel in front of it, is the most popular and well known spot on the island for dunking a live eel with the hopes of catching a big fish. I have heard many different theories as to how the tides impact the fishing at Brant Point, but the hour on both sides of a nocturnal high tide are widely regarded as the best. The boat traffic off Brant Point, even in the spring and fall, is significant, and as a result the fishing is usually not good mid-day when boats are continually passing through the area.

In my own successes with eels, most have come from Sankaty, but a few of them have come from the hole off Second Point. I have had success drifting an eel through the hole and by anchoring on the side of the hole and tossing an eel into it. I usually use a one-ounce weight, on a fishfinder rig, to make the eel consider going to the bottom without hampering its movements too much. However, you may find your eel will dive on its own, therefore no added weight is necessary.

Nantucket Harbor offers a little taste of just about every kind of fishing you can find around the island, and oftentimes it is second to none. Exploring the harbor by boat or on foot is a terrific way to find some fish. You will find flats inside the bends of Coatue that can be approached in the same manner as fishing Madaket Harbor and Tuckernuck, you will find numerous creeks flowing out into the harbor along the south side where bait congregate, thus attracting fish. You will also find shallow sandbars with rushing tide off Pocomo Point and Second Point. Along the shore of Quaise and along the south side of the Head of the Harbor, you will find the rockiest shores on Nantucket. My uncle, Bob Ruley, once a member of the fly-fishing mob that congregated at Jetties, now routinely does some business with stripers of all sizes on spinning and fly gear along the Quaise shore, and his success is not limited just to June, when you can catch stripers almost everywhere on the island. As the summer rolls on, Ruley shifts his trips to after dinner and often finds a pretty good night bite in the area. All these spots are in addition to the fact that the harbor is an excellent spot to find stripers, probably with the help of some birds, busting up bait on the surface.

When you start fishing, and even to some degree when you start fishing a new location, it is easy to subscribe to the thinking that the best fishing and the biggest fish are going to be far away. Sometimes it is easy to equate long runs with good fishing. It is difficult, for whatever reason, to come to the realization that the fishing right under our noses may be just as good if not better. You may be tempted to run your boat around the island to the Old Man Shoal, or battle the big surf of the open Atlantic at Nobadeer; and while those outings can certainly pay off, exploring the tranquil, bait and habitat-filled Nantucket Harbor is certainly worth your consideration.

Flats Fishing

Flats fishing for stripers is no longer a new thing, but I would say it is still a young thing. When I started fly fishing there were people already pursuing stripers in shallow water. The flats of Monomoy Island off Chatham, and to a lesser extent, those of Tuckernuck, were already on the fly-fishing map. Before then, it was very unusual for anglers to pursue striped bass in water less than a few feet deep, and I would venture to say that most anglers didn't even know fish were there. The discovery and subsequent popularity of fishing for striped bass on the flats went hand in hand with the increasing popularity of saltwater fly fishing, both feeding off the other. While it is possible to catch stripers on the fly in any number of situations, there are few opportunities as well suited to fly fishing as you will find on the flats. Fly anglers searching out fish and situations suited to their tackle naturally gravitated to these locations, and the more time anglers spent on the flats, the more fish they discovered, and an exciting fishery was popularized.

Regardless of whether you prefer a spinning rod or fly rod, the flats are a very productive and exciting place to fish. Catching a striped bass anywhere is a lot of fun, but catching one in water a foot or two deep is hard to beat. Size wise, the fish on the flats vary more from fish to fish than anywhere else. If you encounter a school of stripers on the South Shore, or Great Point, or in the harbor, they are usually all of a similar size. But on the flats, you can catch a twenty-inch fish on one cast, and have your next cast hammered by a forty-incher. If really big stripers are what you are after, I would not suggest the flats as the best place for you to start, but do not think of the flats as a place where only schoolies dwell. Over the past few years I have caught two fish over forty inches, and several more approaching forty, in water that was barely deep enough to cover their backs.

The majority of Nantucket's flats fishing takes place near the west end, and you will find most flats guides operating out of Madaket Harbor. Virtually all of Madaket Harbor is grassy flats, and sandy flats extend for miles north and east of Tuckernuck. Shallow water also extends from the shore north and east of Eel Point (these flats are of particular interest to shore bound anglers because no boat is required). Outside of Madaket, there are lots of shallows in Nantucket Harbor that could be considered flats, like the area just north of the Polpis harbor channel mentioned earlier, and at one time or another, almost all of them hold fish. Even if you are not at the bow of a bonefish-style skiff on the sand bottomed flats of Tuckernuck, do not hesitate to fish in any of the shallows you may find.

In my experience, I have not found many fish on the flats until at least a few weeks after they arrive in the spring, and I have consistently had more luck on the flats in Nantucket Harbor early in the spring before there are a lot of fish in Madaket Harbor. I suspect this is because Madaket Harbor is very open to the ocean, whereas town is fairly protected allowing the water to heat up faster.

Flats fishing is at its peak in June. The fish often show up on the flats in May, and usually there are still good numbers on the flats into July. Some stripers remain on the flats through the summer, and flats fishing enthusiasts can be found out there even in the middle of August. Personally I don't spend a lot of time on the flats past mid-July. I would say on an average morning in June, while drifting and poling the flats, it would not be uncommon to see more than one hundred stripers. Many of them you will see only after they've been spooked, and catching them will be impossible, but nonetheless there are a lot of fish present. A morning on the same spots in mid-summer and you will be lucky to see a half dozen fish, and one or two will be more likely. I have found the flats in Madaket Harbor are the first to hold lots of fish, and the Tuckernuck flats tend to stay better longer, even as the number of fish in Madaket harbor decreases. The fish start to move up onto the flats again in very late August and September, but at least in recent seasons, their numbers in the fall do not approach where they were in the spring.

The traditional way to flats fish, first popularized by bonefishermen in the Florida Keys, has spread to many different locations and is used in pursuit of many different species. It involves the angler at the bow of a skiff and a guide or a friend poling the skiff along through shallow water, both of them looking for fish. Stealth is important, and poling, rather than motoring, is essential to get within casting range. When the fish are spotted, the person poling does what he can to get the boat into a good position for the angler to cast. This is certainly an effective way to fish stripers on the flats, but it is not the only way. If you find yourself without a skiff, or a friend to pole you along, there are many other effective ways to successfully fish the flats.

I am often fishing the flats by myself, with nobody to pole or be poled by. When that is the case, I usually go to where I think the fish may be and after making an educated guess as to which direction the wind and the tide will take me, I drift across the area where I intend to fish. Unlike traditional flats sight fishing, where the angler just waits and watches until a fish is sighted to make a cast, I continually blind cast for the vast majority of my time on the flats. Even though it is not quite as romantic as spotting a fish, making a single cast and watching the fish eat, it is quite effective. The numbers of striped bass present in the spring are such that you are certainly not wasting your time, and if there are striped bass sitting still over a grassy bottom the first glimpse you get of them is going to be the swirl they make quickly leaving the area, and you are not going to get a cast to them at all unless you are blind casting.

One very nice aspect of flats fishing is that it can be productive without being too technical. Often times fishing success depends on precision: choosing the right lure, being at the right spot, fishing the right depth, at the right time, etcetera, and if any of those are off, so is the fishing. In a later chapter dealing with striped bass fishing at Great Point, I stress the importance of your lure being within a few specific feet relative to the rip. And while catching fish in shallow water certainly presents some challenges and is by no means easy, at the same time, fishing the flats of Nantucket can be very straightforward and a relatively stress free way to catch some fish.

I offer plenty of detailed strategies and advice in the coming pages to help you fish the flats effectively, but if you are a beginner looking for a straightforward and simple plan that will likely prove effective, here it is: go out in June in a small boat and drift from any side of Madaket Harbor to the other, use a white, six-inch, Hogy, Texas-rigged and weightless (a diagram will follow). Manage to make it look somewhat life-like on the retrieve, and it is likely you'll have a few hits. If you do it early in the morning or in the evening, you will probably have more than a few hits. If you do not like the boat part of that equation, walk around the edges of Madaket Harbor doing the same thing, and you will likely have some success as well.

Now, for those of you who are looking to complicate your fishing lives, I will move on to the finer points. While I advocate blind casting to clients, and I consistently blind cast when fishing the flats on my own, seeing the stripers is certainly an advantage, and while I am casting I am also constantly looking. The flats of Madaket Harbor, for the most part, have a grassy bottom. While it is all but impossible to see the actual fish in or over grass, it is possible to sight fish them. Instead of looking directly into the water, focus your efforts on the surface of the water, and specifically on little wakes created by moving fish. While you will occasionally sight a striper's tail, stripers do not tail as often as other flats gamefish such as bonefish, permit and redfish, so focusing your efforts on locating tails is not going to be fruitful. However, when a striper or a group of stripers swim in shallow water they displace enough water to disrupt the surface in the form of wakes. Sometimes the result is a barely noticeable patch of nervous water and sometimes it is a large wake about as obvious as your boat's. The differences result from a number of conditions: the depth of the water, the proximity of the fish to the surface, the size and number of the fish, and surface conditions (smooth or choppy). In my experience guiding, it is usually more difficult for people to spot this moving water than it is to spot actual fish, though I believe after some time and experience, these wakes are generally easier to spot and can be seen from far greater distances than actual fish in the water. Nothing is going to replace experience for being able to see the wakes created by fish, and even for the most experienced anglers it is always something of a guessing game. Just keep in mind that you are analyzing the surface for idiosyncrasies. It could be little ripples on a glassy morning, or it could be a little patch of seemingly placid water amongst a little chop. It may be a little round area where the waves just seem to be moving in a different direction, and it may be a v-shaped formation of waves that resembles a flock of migrating geese. In any case, if anything appears different, give it closer inspection, and after a pause to give it some inspection, cast to it. The pause is important because if the fish are disturbing the water, they are probably moving, and if they are moving, you want to determine their direction and cast out in front of them, rather than on top of them or behind them. Like most fish in shallow water, striped bass on the flats are fairly nervous and quick to leave when alerted to anything out of the ordinary.

Also keep your eyes out for signs of active feeding, usually in the form of swirls. The swirl of a feeding fish looks pretty much like the swirl of a fish that is leaving because you just drifted over his head, but it is usually faster, more dramatic and louder. The swirls will alert you to the feeding fish, but unlike the wakes of nervous water caused by fish on the move, they will probably not be of any use in determining the fish's current movements. Blanketing the area of the swirl with a series of casts, trying to get your first cast as close as possible to the initial swirl, is the best course of action.

Outside of Madaket Harbor you will find more sandy bottom spots and your focus should shift somewhat toward spotting the actual fish rather than looking for evidence of their movements. There are sandy spots in the harbor, where seeing the fish is possible, and many grassy flats outside the harbor where your focus should be on the surface rather than below it, but spotting wakes and waves becomes a little more difficult. While Madaket Harbor has significant tides the water is comparatively placid. Tidal flow on the Tuckernuck Flats is rapid and depth changes create a series of edges and eddies that can look like moving fish and at the same time confuse and erase many of the wakes actually made by fish.

When you are scanning the sandy bottom for stripers, seeing the fish's shadow is usually much easier than seeing the fish itself. The difference is perhaps minimal, in either case you are scanning the shallows intently looking for an actual fish, but I find it usually helps people zero in on their targets when they know they are more likely to detect the dark shadow moving along the sand than the camouflaged and the reflective sides of the fish in the water column.

Despite two memorable exceptions, birds are not a tremendous help in locating fish on the flats. Birds tend to really get in on the action when the feeding is frenzied and baitfish are being corralled and herded to the top, whereas the flats offer striped bass more of a casual buffet. The first exception occurred one morning in June of 2010 when Mike Schuster, my mate onboard the *Topspin* and accomplice in chasing fish even when we are not working, and I arrived early on the flats. I caught a couple smallish fish on the fly but otherwise it had been slow. We drove over to inspect a group of terns hitting the water over a grassy little flat just east of Tuckernuck for a quick last look before heading back to the dock. After our arrival we quickly saw the very, very large swirls happening with some regularity all over the little flat, and we proceeded to start fishing in a panic. I had handed the fly rod off to Mike and was fishing a Hogy. After an enthusiastic take and a long and powerful run my first fish snapped the hook (probably not my fault), and after another encouraging bite and a big run, the second fish left me with nothing but a leader with little curly q's indicative of a rushed and poor knot (definitely my fault). Mike had several close calls on the fly, but none resulted in landing a fish. As the birds were beginning to depart, and the swirls were becoming few and far between, I managed to land one thirty-incher, which I am certain was significantly smaller than both of the previous hooked fish, but it was better than getting totally blanked after stumbling into several large stripers actively feeding.

The second instance happened one morning on the flats when I motored over to inspect a huge group of seagulls hitting the water. I could see a bunch of stripers taking advantage of what looked to be some kind of crab hatch. They were all eagerly stacked up in one of the little edges off Tuckernuck picking off little crustaceans as they were swept over the edge. I caught a couple stripers on a little plastic crab imitation that has proved ineffective every other time I have used it. In all my time on the flats I have never seen anything like this before or since. As a general rule, any heavy bird activity is probably worth investigation, but on the flats, your time will be much better spent analyzing the surface and below rather than trying to spot birds.

In addition to looking for fish, pay attention to the bottom when you are on the flats. Differences in the bottom will often hold fish, and this is the case no matter what the difference is. For instance, if there is a depression in the flat, there will often be a few sitting in it, and if there is a hump, some fish may be on top of it or near it. Moving fish will often travel along transition lines, whether that transition is along a drop-off, or from grassy to sandy bottom (it is often the case that both transitions take place at once). If the flat is predominantly grassy, sometimes the fish will lie in sandy spots, and if the flat is sandy, the fish may be using any available grass as an ambush point. If the bottom of a particular area is patchy, with some grass, some sand, and some holes, that entire area is worth some attention.

Given the goal of this guide is to be detailed, local and specific, I will mention some areas on the west end flats that have become favorites of mine over the years, but I will caution you against putting in a lot of effort seeking them out. You are going to find that you will have much more success concentrating on finding fish and the features that attract fish talked about in the preceding paragraphs, rather than devoting any time or energy trying to seek out a specific few square yards of flat where I once caught some fish. In the grass-bottom dominated Madaket Harbor, there are a few sandy patches west of Eel Point, just south of the channel, that are excellent places to find a few fish. I always associate those sandy patches with one of the most beautiful and visual takes I have ever had. A couple years ago, I was out on the flats for the first time that season in late May, and I had set up my drift to take me close to the sandy patches. I saw a couple fish cruise over the sand on the far edge, and I made a cast. I remember the fish immediately coming back out over the sand, and with the afternoon sun I would not have seen him more clearly if he was inches away from me in a tank. He followed my Hogy most of the way back with neither apprehension nor urgency, and then as I sped up my retrieve he abandoned his casual pace, darting forward to slurp down my lure. A good example of everything going just right.

There is a channel coming out of the cove on Esther's Island that is several feet deeper than the surrounding water that often holds some fish, and just northeast of that channel there is a patchy area of grass and little sand holes that often holds some fish. If there is a sandy cut in the bottom surrounded by grassy flats, the fish will often hold on the edges. There is a large flat that wraps around the eastern corner of Tuckernuck, just northeast of the harbor, which has become a particular favorite of mine in the last couple years, and its defining feature is sandy cuts through a grassy bottom. While at one time or another I have caught fish on just about every part of the flat, I have always had the most consistent success on the edges of the cuts. The tide really zips over this flat, and the stripers often sit on the edges of the cuts, sometimes visible over the sand and sometimes hidden just in the edges of the grass, and they feed on whatever food items come down the cut. While I will address tackle and fishing methods for the flats shortly, I will touch on a specialized method that I have found effective at this spot, and similar cuts on flats with a lot of current. An effective offering for this situation is to fish a crab fly much like you would fish a nymph for trout. My own nymph fishing experience is miniscule, but on the rare occasions that I have done it, my immediate thought was, "Hey, this is like fishing crab flies in the strong tide off Tuckernuck." From a stationary boat, or standing in the water (be careful, the tide is strong) just throw the fly up-tide into the cut and the tide will do the work, just strip to take up the slack and perhaps, especially if you are a competent trout angler, throw a mend or two into the line to extend your effective drift. Unlike nymph fishing, it is not necessary to have a precise and perfect drift unaffected by anything but the current on your fly. If your fly dances a little bit, or the current on your line sweeps it a little quicker, it just imitates a struggling crab rather than a passive one and the stripers don't mind. Do not hesitate to strip a little bit here and there to adjust your drift. If all goes well, a striper will be sitting on the edge of the cut, mistake your fly for a crab caught in the current, and zip out to inhale it. If conditions are right, you can watch your fly's progress down the cut and then watch the fish come out to eat, but doing it all by feel is also effective.

Fishing around creek mouths, particularly on the falling tide, a method I find particularly productive in Nantucket Harbor in the spring, can also be very effective on the flats. The creek that enters Madaket Harbor on the south side of Eel Point, the entrance to the cove on Esther's Island, around the mouth of Hither Creek, and the creek flowing out of the Bathtub on the north side of Eel Point are all good places to find fish.

The flats northeast of Eel Point, and those to the north and east of Tuckernuck are the predominately sandy ones, and hence your best option for seeing the fish first, and then presenting a fly or lure.

Soft plastic stick baits, such as Hogys and Slug-gos, are excellent choices for the flats. I use a white, six-inch skinny Hogy, Texas rigged and weightless, about ninety percent of the time. They are my first choice for two reasons, the first being that they are weedless when rigged Texas style. There is often eelgrass or other vegetation floating on or in the water, which will quickly sully your offering, even if it is a topwater, and the water is so shallow it is difficult at times to keep a subsurface offering out of the weeds on the bottom. The next reason is the lure's action. An unweighted Hogy's movements are wonderfully erratic, sliding across the top of the water, diving several inches under the water, even popping out of the water on occasion. A striper in very shallow water may be put off or startled by a loud, hard plastic topwater offering, but a soft plastic seems to create just enough commotion to draw their attention while still retaining some qualities of a sand eel or other natural bait. A fish that may not be sufficiently aggressive to launch an attack on a big, bubbling plug will often be moved to inhale a Hogy.

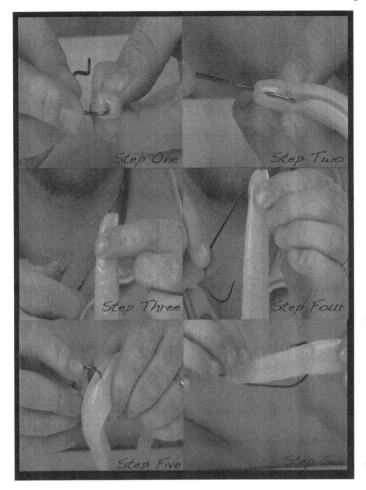

Texas Rigging A Hogy

- Step 1: Line the bait up with the hook and eye ball placement where the hook will enter and exit the bait. (You can mark each spot with a permanent marker.) The idea here is to make sure the hook will lay perfectly straight inside the bait once it's rigged.
- Step 2: Pass the hook through the center of the bait's nose, and exit where you eyeballed proper placement.
- Step 3: Rotate the hook, so the hook gap is facing the top of the bait, usually the flat portion and insert the hook into the back of the bait, down the centerline.

Optional Step 4: Bury the hook point so that it cannot pick up weeds.

reprinted with permission from www.hogylures.com

Over the years I have tried other colors, and caught some fish on both solid black, and the hot color of the last two seasons, solid pink. While there were a handful of days that the fish exhibited a slight preference for black or pink, they are the exception rather than the rule. By way of example, I buy white Hogys by the case, and I occasionally pick up a bag of black or pink. Occasionally, on a high tide, or if the fish seem to be sitting in the deeper cuts, I will add a small bullet weight to the leader in front of the hook. It eliminates the attractive topwater aspect of the lure, but the erratic action and weedless qualities remain, and on some days bringing your offering down to the fish will prove effective.

Hogys can be effectively retrieved in a number of ways. For fishing unweighted ones on the flats, I find an erratic retrieve works best. Twitch your rod tip and then take in the slack at varied intervals. For example, I will give three twitches, followed by a short pause, and another twitch, followed by a pause, and two twitches. I favor a quick retrieve, but experiment and see what the fish prefer. Sometimes you will see a fish following your lure (either a wake or the fish itself) and at that point you may be tempted to slow or stop your retrieve. To avoid this remember that fish are fast swimmers. If they are not eating your lure, it is assuredly not because they are not quick enough to catch it. Stopping your lure gives the fish a better look at it, and may alert them that something is out of the ordinary. Upon learning a striper is behind it, a real baitfish will probably flee as fast as possible, and emulating this with your lure will work to your advantage. When I see a fish following my lure, I immediately speed up my retrieve. Often, as the lure starts moving faster, the fish will immediately become excited, commit to eating it, and dramatically increase their own pace. Once they are in hot pursuit, rather than just examining your lure, then a well-timed pause in your retrieve will let them eat it.

A drawback to soft plastics is casting distance. While their lightness is what gives them their erratic action and seductive topwater appeal, it certainly does not help you lob the thing out. Using a rod designed to throw light lures certainly helps. If you find your rod too heavy to throw the 6 inchers, the lures get significantly heavier going up in size and they are still very effective.

Traditional topwater plugs are very effective on the flats. They trigger ferocious strikes, and they are often the answer to manufacturing a few bites on tough days. Their weight and bulk allows you cast them very far and cover a lot of ground. If you are a beginning caster, they are easier to learn with than a lighter lure.

Slow sinking plugs and suspending twitch baits can be very effective, and I usually have a few of the Mirrolure Catch Series in my box. Small molded plastics like Storm Minnows are a good option too.

For fly fishing, the tried and true classic, Lefty's Deceiver, has always been my top producer. I tie most of mine with green and black barred feathers and a chartreuse back. Any sand eel imitation is a good choice, and weedless Clousers are also very effective. Recently, I spent a morning redfishing with Capt. Greg McKee around Pine Island, Florida, and he introduced me to a very popular pattern there, the Gurgler. One of my first thoughts was that it would be a great fly for stripers on the flats. My introduction to the fly on the flats of Southwest Florida is particularly ironic because in my research I found the fly was created for stripers by Boston fly fisherman and master fly tier, Jack Gartside. I am not sure how I have come this far without running into one before, but rest assured, my box is now well stocked with Gurglers for next season.

My Favorite Striper Flies

Top to Bottom: Jack Gartside's Gurgler, Lefty's Deceiver with chartreuse and black barred feathers, Chunky Sand Eel with a blue back, Chunky Sand Eel with a green back, Clouser Minnow, Squid imitation, Crab Fly

There is no denying that stripers on the flats eat a lot of crabs. Crab imitations popularized in permit fishing are very effective. I like using a crab imitation when sight fishing over sandy flats. Crabs are very good choices to throw into the path of striper, or group of stripers, and let them sit, and give them a couple little strips when the fish approach. As mentioned earlier, I also like drifting crabs in the nymph-like method through cuts in the flat, but for blind casting or fishing over grassy bottom, I prefer streamers. Casting and stripping in a streamer is exactly what you want to do to give it the proper action, and your retrieve is going to be largely similar whether you can see the fish or not. While you certainly can have success casting a crab fly blindly and slowly stripping it in, I always find myself lacking confidence when I am doing this, and having confidence in your own offering is important.

SUMMERTIME STRIPERS

While it is not the wide-open bite of June, there are still plenty of stripers to be had in the height of summer. Two very basic starting points to help you find stripers in the summer are to fish later and to fish deeper. Stripers that spent some big chunks of daylight feeding in June may become almost totally nocturnal in July and August. As for finding fish in the daytime, the harbors and flats will no longer be a great option; a boat will be helpful and plying the deeper waters of Sankaty and the eastern rips are your best option. Also, be prepared to ignore conventional advice from time to time, including that which I just gave you. Striped bass may prefer the cooler waters of spring and fall, but they are a resilient fish that thrive in many water temperatures whose movements are often driven by bait more than temperature. The new world record 81 pounder of 2011 was caught in tepid Long Island Sound, and while it was caught using the traditional advice to fish at night, the traditional wisdom of fishing for stripers in the spring and fall was ignored, and the fish was caught on August 4th. When fishing onboard the *Topspin*, it is rare for a mid-summer week to go by without some clients telling me they watched a nearby angler catch a striper while they sunbathed on the beach. Certainly, a mid-day fish from the surf is probably the result of luck more than anything else, but a striper caught nonetheless. The following section about striper fishing at Great Point is about fishing for daytime stripers in very shallow water, and it is often at its peak in mid-July.

Great Point Striper Fishing

If you needed to name a bluefish capital of Nantucket, Great Point would likely top your list. It is the standard location for downtown charter boats on their common 2½-hour trips, it is the most well-known and well-attended surf fishing location (when it is open), and is often the choice of recreational boaters. The lighthouse among the dunes makes for beautiful scenery, but below the surface, Great Point is equally impressive. Nantucket Sound is west of the point, and the Atlantic Ocean is to the east. Starting at the tip of the point a shoal runs northeast then turns east and runs a couple miles out into the Atlantic. On the Nantucket Sound side and continuing North of the shoal, the water is some of the deepest around the island, with depths between forty and seventy feet. Within a cast's length, the shoal shoots up nearly vertically to within a few feet of the surface. At low tide some of the spots are nearly exposed; there is about four to six of water in the deeper cuts, and the average along most of the edge is about three feet. As you head south over the edge along Nantucket's eastern shore toward Sankaty, the depths increase more gradually to between fifteen to thirty feet largely dependent on how far east of the island you are. When the tide is running, both in and out, a powerful rip is formed over the shoal.

Great Point's reputation as a bluefish hot spot is certainly well deserved, but it is often overlooked as a spot to find stripers. The best time to fish Great Point for stripers is on the incoming (or east) tide. A series of little edges form, with the shallowest part of the shoal being right out in front of the edge, and the fish sit along that edge, holding themselves in place against the current and waiting for small baitfish to be delivered to them via the tide. All of the water and all of the bait in the seventy adjacent feet is trying to squeeze over the shoal, and it creates a golden feeding opportunity for the fish, and a golden angling opportunity for you.

It was at Great Point, and not the flats or the outer rips, that I enjoyed my best day of fly-rod striped bass fishing ever. In late June of 2011 Mike Schuster and I were headed back from a good morning off Sankaty with clients onboard *Topspin*, when we heard some chatter over the radio that a couple of the boats trolling for bluefish that morning at Great Point had gotten a handful of stripers as well. Now, the boats involved are not known for light tackle or stealth, and Mike and I suspected that if they got a handful of stripers, there must be a pile of them there. We hoped that by targeting them with lighter tackle, we might really crush them. In another fine example of everything working out just right, the next day a nice east tide would be running at the Point at daylight, light winds were forecast, and our schedule allowed us to sneak out for a few hours on our own in the morning. The next morning at first light we loaded a couple light spinning rods and our fly rods and headed out. It was not light enough to see the fish when we first arrived, but Mike threw a Hogy into the edge and it was quickly inhaled by a striper. After getting that fish, we both picked up fly rods and cast as we drifted through the edge. They exhibited their usual pickiness even toward flies, but after a couple different tries, we found they were really turned on by a chunky green-backed sand-eel imitation I tied in the surf candy style. After we arrived at the right fly, almost every well-placed cast was eaten, and we proceeded to catch enough fish to lose count, but I would guess it was about seven or eight each. One of us would get one just about every drift through the edge, and plenty of times we were both on. None of the fish were huge, but they were all quality fish up to about thirty-five inches. We left them biting in order to be at the dock in time for our charter. Mike and I never made it back on our own that season, always having interested customers to take with us. That is certainly not a bad thing, but I would be lying if I told you I wasn't looking forward to going back with Mike and our fly rods next season in order to "check things out."

If the stripers are in the rip at Great Point they can often be seen sitting right on the shallowest part, just in front of the edge. When I am running the *Topspin*, I have the advantage of a tower, and the extra height certainly helps, but the bottom is sandy and shallow and usually a tower is not necessary to see the fish. Seeing the fish certainly helps, but you can effectively target them without seeing them.

While stealth is certainly called for, if you get too close to the fish and they spook, it is usually not catastrophic for two reasons. The first being that fish in a rip, even a shallow one, are much more resilient to being spooked than fish on the flats. If you drift over them and they scatter, they will probably return to the edge to continue feeding shortly after you drift through. That is not to say that you can continually come close to them with impunity; the first fish to totally vamoose will probably be the biggest ones and you certainly do not want that. The fish, usually fickle in terms of your offering to begin with, will probably become wearier with each pass, and enough motoring or drifting over their spot will eventually cause them to abandon it altogether. The next reason not to be terribly concerned with alerting one group of fish to your presence is that there are dozens of edges made up as you head eastward along the shoal. More often than not, if there are stripers in one of the edges they will also be in another, and when fishing is good they will be in most of them.

Many of the edges are similar in appearance, and if you do spot some fish (or spook them) be sure to note their location. They will probably be sitting in the same location relative to the next edge. That is to say, if they are stacked up in front of the northern corner of one edge in the shallow water, they are probably stacked up off the northern corner of the next edge in shallow water. If you see some fish or get a bite just behind one edge, be sure to look closely and work some casts just behind the next edge. Noting the location of fish on one edge will help you spot the fish and pinpoint your casts on the next edge.

I tend to fish Great Point for stripers in two distinct ways. Most often I am there with clients, and I am driving the boat while they cast. Having someone constantly at the helm is very effective, and even if there are only two of you fishing, one person fishing and one person driving will probably be more successful than if you were to both fish, at least until you get a feel for exactly where the fish are. When driving, I try to keep the boat almost stationary about one easy cast length north of the edge, or sometimes, letting the current push me east along the edge while staying north of it. The anglers try to keep their lures in the zone that is producing bites through casting, retrieving and dropping back. The tidal flow is such that if the lure is stationary, it will appear to be moving and if it dropped back by free spooling it will be quickly sucked over the edge. My offering of choice is the same as it is on the flats: a white Hogy, rigged weedless and unweighted. At Great Point, I usually start with the seven inch size, but some days the fish seem to prefer the six inchers. Once the Hogy is where you want it, just a light twitching of the rod tip usually imparts the right action.

Most often the fish are right on the edge or within about three feet out in front of it sitting right on the shallowest part. When the fish are there, the fishing is extremely visual and especially from my perch in the tower I can direct the lures through instructions to retrieve or drop back until they are right in front of the fish. Even without the benefit of a bird's eye view it is easy to see the edge and keep your offering right in it or in front of it.

Fishing a few feet behind the edge can be effective as well. It will be difficult to spot the fish there unless they are actively busting bait, but often times they are there. The fish that sit in the shallowest spots out in front of the edge and notoriously picky about what they eat, and sometimes even with a light fluorocarbon leader and a Hogy you cannot get them to bite. When that is the case, I will try fishing behind the visible fish, behind the edge. Although I can't see the fish, there are often a few sitting there that will bite when their visible schoolmates in front of them seem to have lockjaw. I suspect that the turbidity of the water behind the edge probably decreases visibility, making the fish unaware of your presence and making your offering a little harder to identify as an imposter, but perhaps the stripers behind the edge are a little less picky because all they have to choose from is what gets by the visible fish in front of them.

Once the angler, or perhaps two if things are hot, is hooked up, slip the boat into neutral and drift back through the edge while fighting the fish. Try not to drift right over the area where the fish are sitting, which is usually

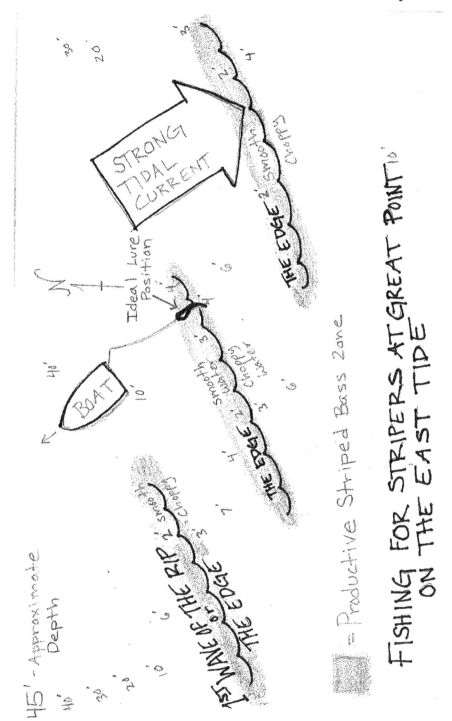

= Productive Striped Bass Zone

FISHING FOR STRIPERS AT GREAT POINT ON THE EAST TIDE

fairly easy because the tide will carry you quickly to the east as well as the south.

When stripers are stacked up in the shallow edges of Great Point, it can make for absolutely fantastic action, and it is possible to put up big numbers that would be all but impossible on the flats. It does, however, require precision. It is exactly the kind of detail-oriented fishing that can result in one boat catching fish after fish while a nearby boat goes home confused and empty handed.

Low profile rigging and lure choice are important, but the most important aspect is lure placement. Blind casting in the general vicinity of Great Point is likely to yield you nothing, or perhaps if you are lucky, a few bluefish. To target stripers effectively, you need to keep your offerings within a few feet of the edge, on either side, and you need to keep them there as long as possible. Additionally, keeping your boat out of that same area, at least for the minutes leading up to fishing there, is very important.

Even if you are fishing on an overcast day at sunrise with no hope of spotting a fish, the edges are still easily visible and fishing the edges precisely and keeping your lure right on it, right in front of it, or right behind it, should yield some bites.

This trolling-casting hybrid method with one person constantly at the wheel is a very effective way to keep your offerings within the productive area for a significant period of time. The current is strong and difficult, but by having the angler constantly adjusting the position of the lures while the person at the helm stems the tide and keeps the boat stationary, it is possible to get your lures precisely where they need to be and keep them there until you get a bite. When your lure is too far in front of the edge, it can merely be dropped back, and if the lure is behind the edge it can be retrieved or the boat can be inched forward. Anchoring the boat could have a similar effect, but anchoring at Great Point is, at best, a tricky proposition, and at worst very dangerous because of the unpredictable swells and strong currents. Pulling a big fish through the edge to an anchored boat on light tackle is nearly impossible and you would waste a lot of fishing time by being locked into one edge each time you anchored. Safety as well as local etiquette strongly discourage anchoring at Great Point.

The other way I fish Great Point on the east tide for stripers is to exclusively cast to them, usually when I am alone or fly fishing. I run the boat north and a little west of where the fish are (or where I think they are), running the distance of one long cast plus a little extra away from the edge. I shut down the motor, and begin to fish with the first cast almost straight toward the edge, retrieved back away from it. As you drift closer to the edge, your casts should become more parallel to it, allowing your lure or fly to spend a greater amount of time in the zone where the fish are feeding, and as you pass over the edge you will still have time for one or two effective casts back toward the edge. If everything is timed correctly, you should have one cast that is fished almost entirely along the edge, where your first and last casts will only be on the edge for a short time.

The current will be very swift and getting your timing down will take some practice. I would recommend fishing a single edge as long as it takes for you to get the timing and positioning down, rather than move to a new edge and alert the fish there to your presence before you have fine-tuned your approach. When fly fishing, plan on four good casts per drift: one as you approach the edge, one when you are almost on it, one when you have just passed it, and one back toward it as you drift past. If spin fishing, it is certainly possible to squeeze in a few more casts, but either way count on quick drifts and a lot of driving the boat. As you drift back across the edge, remember that on your first cast or two a speedy retrieve will be necessary because the boat will be bearing down on your lure or fly very quickly caus-ing much of your retrieve to be spent just picking up slack, and once you get past the edge you just need to impart a little action, because the current will be effectively trolling your offering. Be aware of what the current is doing to your retrieve, because while sometimes the fish will hit a fly or Hogy drifting in the tide, they certainly prefer a little action and you do not want to execute everything else perfectly only to have your fly drift lifelessly by a striper.

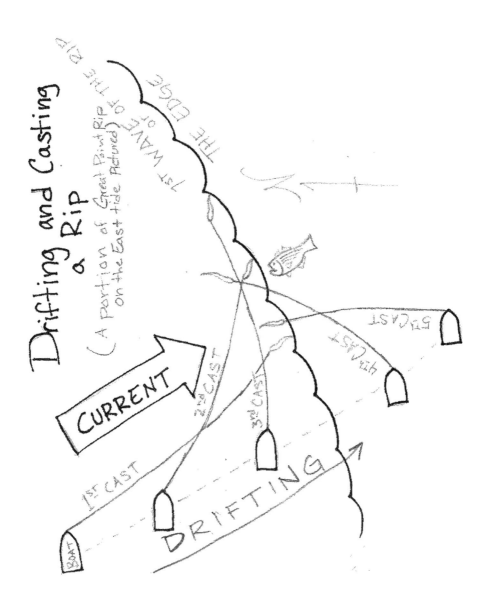

Drifting and Casting a Rip

(A portion of Great Point Rip the 2 on the East tide Pictured) of 1st WAVE of 2nd

THE EDGE

CURRENT

3RD CAST

2ND CAST

1ST CAST

3RD CAST

4TH CAST

5TH CAST

BOAT

DRIFTING

When fishing Great Point with Hogys on twenty-five or thirty pound fluorocarbon leaders, you are going to lose some tackle to bluefish and their vicious teeth. Although this is largely the case anywhere and everywhere around Nantucket, at Great Point you can fly through a bag of Hogys, a package of hooks, and spool of leader in no time. As I stated earlier, Great Point is the well-deserved bluefish capital of Nantucket and while both late spring and early summer (late June through mid-July) in 2010 and 2011 produced a lopsided ratio of stripers to blues, more often than not, there will be some bluefish around. While bluefish are certainly not without virtue, I am seldom happy to have one eat a Hogy tied to a fluorocarbon leader, which can result in anything from a half a Hogy to a mess of shredded leader, and rarely results in a caught fish. Luckily, keeping your lure very close to the edge in the area where you are most likely to get a striper is also the best way to avoid bluefish. If conditions dictate fishing behind the edge, do not let your lure get more than a couple feet behind it. While bluefish certainly stack up and feed in the edge at times, in mid-June through mid-July on the east tide the stripers are often tight to the edge while the bluefish are cruising the area more randomly.

If the bluefish are thick and mixed right in with the stripers, switch your lure to something more durable. A needlefish, a slender and durable topwater that stands up well to repeated bluefish attacks, would be my next choice. Deadly Dicks and swimming plugs can also be effective. Continue to rig with monofilament or fluorocarbon leaders, although I may beef them up a little. Also consider replacing the standard little treble hooks on all of the above lures with a beefier single hook in the rear. I find that fish tend to stay buttoned up better with a big single hook and if rigged in this manner, the lure itself will protect your leader from the destructive teeth of bluefish.

If you are fly fishing, the aforementioned chunky sand eel is my favorite. Deceivers and other baitfish imitations are good options. Clouser Minnows and similar flies, especially tied in with a sand eel in mind, can have great results and you do not need to worry about your fly snagging or picking up weeds from the bottom because the bottom is pure sand.

While the tide is by far the most important factor when fishing for stripers on a Great Point rip, time of day is a factor as well as weather conditions. When the east tide coincides with sunrise, fishing is likely to be at its best. I am much more of a sunrise fisherman than a sunset one, but the lower light in the evening can also get the fish a little more active. I have caught plenty of stripers off Great Point in very shallow water under a mid-day sun shining in July, but they tend to bite a little better when it gets a little overcast or the light goes down a little bit. This is the *Catch 22* of almost all sight fishing in that as the light disappears, the fish can become difficult or impossible to spot, but they are less spooky and bite better. On overcast days, I am hoping for a little sunshine in order to see the fish, and on sunny days, I am hoping for some clouds to pass by so the fish I am looking at will bite.

The east tide is preferred for striper fishing at Great Point, but there are certainly stripers to be had on the west (outgoing) tide as well. While on the east tide it is usually possible to target stripers exclusively by sight fishing and using very light gear, it is almost impossible to use the same approach on the west tide, and using any kind of gear that can't stand up to bluefish is not advisable. While oftentimes the striped bass will have the shallow edges of the east tide all to themselves, it is rare that bluefish are not present right in the slightly deeper edges of the west tide. The effective way to find stripers at Great Point on the west tide usually means fishing the edge and being prepared for a mixed bag of blues and stripers. In a later chapter on bluefish, I will discuss trolling and casting for them at Great Point, and the standard lures are large orange plastic squid, locally called hoochies, for trolling and chunky poppers such as ballistic missiles for casting. If you want to try and add a few stripers to your catch, try changing your offering. I usually troll a white parachute jig with a pork rind (the same lure traditionally used when wire-lining but fished on monofilament or dacron line because Great Point is such a shallow rip) or cast or troll a Pearl Bomber rigged on a heavy mono or fluorocarbon leader (eighty pound test is a good starting point). Both choices will stand up well to bluefish, and they are both effective at fooling any stripers that may be mixed in the edge with them.

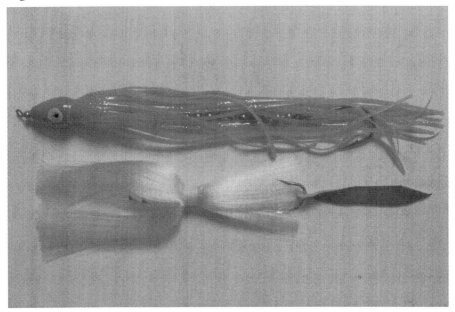

Essentials for Nantucket Trolling

Orange Hoochie (top) and White Parachute Jig with a red Uncle Josh's Pork Rind (bottom)

For the most part, on the west tide the eastern part of the rip tends to hold more stripers than the portion close to land, but the entire area is worth investigating.

Great Point offers a unique opportunity in that the fish are actively feeding in a rip and the rip is only a few feet deep. While it is not on par with Sankaty as a productive striper spot day-in and day-out all season, in 2010 and 2011 there was good fishing for several weeks in June and July. If you are able to take advantage of it, it is exciting way to catch stripers in a dynamic spot.

Sankaty and the Eastern Shore of Nantucket

The deep, cool waters just east of Sankaty Head are some of the most consistent and productive around Nantucket for finding and catching stripers. The fish arrive off Sankaty in late May or early June and stay until October or perhaps November. Of course there are a few "should have been here yesterday" days when the fishing totally shuts down, the type of days when theories and conjectures are prevalent but answers are few and far between, but usually the waters off Sankaty are a great place to find striped bass.

Obviously, some times are better than others, with June, early July and September usually being better than the height of summer. That being said, if you want to catch a striped bass in the middle of August and the rips east of Nantucket are not an option, Sankaty is almost surely your best bet. Even at mid-day on the hottest days of August it is possible to find a few hungry stripers at Sankaty.

The bottom of Sankaty is often referred to as "cobble bottom," and compared to the sandy bottom surrounding most of Nantucket, it holds a lot of life. Unlike fishing a rip, where you can often times identify with some precision where the fish are, and where your lure is likely to be attacked, finding fish at Sankaty is little more random. It is not unlike looking for a needle in a haystack, although hopefully there are lots of needles, they are usually found in bunches, and sometimes they will be where you found them last time.

Virtually all of the water from Sankaty Light south to the Old Man Shoal, north to Great Point and east a couple miles is productive at one time or another, and all of that water can be approached in a similar way. In the interest of narrowing the search area, I will give you a not wholly groundless opinion that the most consistently productive area lies directly east of the lighthouse in depths of twenty to thirty-five feet and not more than a half-mile North or a mile South.

For several years in the late 1990s and early 2000s, usually in the middle of summer, you could find schools of big striped bass about halfway between Great Point and Sankaty in the area off Wauwinet. These fish were often in the forty-inch range. The area quickly became a favorite of commercial bass fisherman, some from Nantucket and many running over from Cape Cod. The particular body of fish that could be found there got hammered pretty badly and the fishing quickly tapered off. Many fisherman stop and look on their way to Sankaty, and occasionally you will find some fish there, but there have not been any schools of big fish off Wauwinet for a couple years. I mention this for three reasons. First, it is a solid tangible example of the striped bass population decline of the past few years being real and impacting fishing. Second, both commercial and recreational fishermen are currently experiencing a similar bounty of large, mid-summer fish off Chatham, and if things don't change, those fish are going to be gone shortly as well. Third, I am optimistic that regulations in Massachusetts, and more importantly nationwide (being that the fish are migratory and there is no such thing as a Massachusetts striper) will improve, the population will climb again, and someday in the future the waters off Wauwinet will again be a great place to find a big cow in mid-summer.

Wire-line trolling is the standard method for fishing Sankaty and the eastern shore, and it is highly effective. The local standard wire line set up is a conventional reel filled with Dacron backing attached to 150 feet of stainless trolling wire, to a monofilament leader anywhere from five to ten feet connected to a four or six ounce white parachute jig, with a red Uncle Josh's pork rind attached. This combination of components is so successful that when local charter captains head to Sankaty, more often than not, every single rod they plan to fish is rigged in this manner. If you are getting started, or rigging up a rod with the intention of fishing Sankaty, or wire lining anywhere around Nantucket for that matter, I would recommend the above set-up. That is not to say that you won't catch fish on anything else; sometimes the fish seem to prefer red or green parachute jigs to white. Other times stripers will crush the big tube lures that have become popular all over New England and will ignore parachutes. The locally preferred one hundred fifty feet of wire is short compared to most wire-line set-ups, but much of the productive water at Sankaty and other areas around Nantucket is around twenty feet and more wire is a liability rather than an asset. However, having more than 150 feet of wire can be helpful especially of you are fishing the deeper waters off Sankaty of thirty and forty feet.

While certainly effective, wire line is not without its difficulties. Oftentimes when people hear "wire-line" they think it is some kind of unbreakable cable, when in fact it is fickle, shockingly delicate, and difficult to work with. Its only advantage is that is sinks. It is easily weakened by kinks or twists, it is prone to tangling and backlashes, and once it is somehow damaged, there is no fixing it, you have to throw it away. Attaching the wire to the backing is a constant problem, and no particular solution is foolproof. An Albright knot is a fairly good option. It is small and fits through guides nicely, but it does weaken the line significantly and over time the wire will cut through the knot or the wire inside the knot will break. It also does not allow for line twisting, but using a swivel to attach your leader can mitigate this problem to a degree. Another option is a small swivel attached to the wire with a haywire twist and then to the backing with a clinch knot or any type of line-to-hardware knot of the angler's preference. The haywire twist is more durable than the bent wire in the Albright knot and it does allow for line twisting, but having a swivel buried on your spool can lead to tangles, and having it go through the guides can be bad. Losing a wire line due to an Albright knot is no fun and if a fish is attached it can even be a minor tragedy, but if a swivel starts popping off your rod guides it is probably going to be a major expense. While there is no perfect method, either will work, and if you take the time to retie your knots every few trips, you can keep your tackle (and fish) losses to a minimum.

There are a couple tips and techniques, some of which are almost essential to your success, and others that may not be necessary at all, but I will touch on them here anyway. First and most importantly, keep in mind that most of the time stripers at Sankaty will be very tight to the bottom, and if your lure isn't very close to or on the bottom, you are not going to get many bites. You want to fine-tune your trolling speed and how much line you let out to keep your lures close the bottom, but as a starting point, if you let out 150 feet of wire, and about thirty feet of backing, and are trolling about three knots, you will probably be pretty close. If you let out more line, you will be able to feel your jig bouncing on the bottom, and this is not always a bad thing. Stripers will happily attack a jig that is bouncing along the bottom and many times bouncing your jig will attract or excite fish that would have let it pass by unmolested only a foot or two above their heads. The problem is that a jig bounced on the bottom will often catch seaweed or some kind of muck, or get hung up. This has become more of a problem recently as homeowners on Sankaty Bluff used sandbags in their attempt to fight erosion. In a totally foreseeable occurrence, many of the bags have ended up in the water, and in addition to destroying bits of the valuable underwater Sankaty habitat; they are very effective at hooking lures.

If you feel your lure bouncing and have not had a strike in some time it is worth checking out, conversely, if the guy in boat next to you is catching fish, and there are fish on your fish finder and you aren't getting bites, try letting your line out a little bit to bounce your jig a few times. The person at the helm watching the fish finder can also accomplish this by slipping the boat into neutral for a few seconds.

You will have more success trolling with the tide than against it. Fish lay with their nose into the tide, letting food get swept to them. If you are trolling with the tide, your lures will be headed at fish and while under most circumstances having your lure charging directly toward a predator is not usually recommended, it is far better than having it approach the fish from behind. Additionally, trolling with the tide helps keep your lure near the bottom, and trolling against it swings your lure up in the water column significantly. When fishing Sankaty, it is likely that some of the other boats will be trolling in one direction, then reeling in and steaming in the other direction in order to troll with the tide again. It is sort of a labor intensive and hectic thing to do, but it is certainly effective. Trolling perpendicular to the tide can also be very effective, and if you are on a trip where bluefish are a pleasant, hard fighting, gamefish rather than a nuisance, trolling in any direction will produce bites. Often, once I get a bite and have waited a minute or so for additional bites, I will work the boat around and idle against the tide while the fish is fought so I do not get swept too far north or south by the tide. However, I do not hesitate to reel in and run up-tide if necessary. Trying to troll back around fish against the tide can waste a lot of valuable time, and you never know how long the fish will stay put and remain hungry.

The last crucial factor involved in catching stripers on wire line is jigging. In addition to the steady movement of the lure being trolled, bouncing your rod back and forth is essential to getting bites. Bouncing the rod imparts the jig with the stop and start motion of a real squid, and it causes the jig to raise and then sink in the water column, covering more ground. I have been fishing wire line at Sankaty for about a decade and half now, and I would say that someone jigging effectively will get about ten times more bites than someone not jigging, and probably about five times more bites than someone jigging lackadaisically.

To jig effectively, once your line is out, move your rod tip several feet, either up or out. Once you have brought the tip up, drop it immediately back down. You want to drop it down fast enough that slack is immediately created and the parachute can fall freely, but you don't want to drop it so fast that a big loop of loose line is created that could potentially find it's was around your rod tip. Once the line is tight again, immediately bring it back up. When thinking about a clock face, straight over your head being twelve,a good motion is from about ten to eleven. Never go all the way to twelve or past it because it will increase the likelihood of wrapping the line around the tip of your rod and it will not improve the motion of your lure at all. The likelihood of breaking the rod tip is pretty good after twelve depending on the boat you are on. Finally, if a fish bites when you are at twelve, you will be in a very awkward position to try and keep a tight line.

Bites come at all times during the jigging, and the key to keeping fish hooked up is to keep the line tight after the bite. Because you are already jigging, and because a common natural reaction to a bite is to jerk back, a common mistake people make once they feel a bite is to attempt to set the hook by making motions similar to their jigging motion. Dropping the rod in order to set the hook gives the fish slack at a critical time, and they are often able to rid themselves of the lure at that moment. Once you feel a bite, just raising your rod slightly and keeping it there is far more effective than dropping your tip in order to get into position to set the hook. The movement of the boat will go a long way toward setting the hook, and getting a few turns on the reel will also set the hook while avoiding loosening the line. If your jigging motion is kept below the eleven o'clock position and you get a bite at the top of your jigging, you still have room to raise your tip slightly to keep the tension on the fish and get a few cranks.

I have always found jigging sideways to be as effective as an up and down motion. The motion and tactics are the same, just turned on their side. Nine o'clock would be straight behind the boat and twelve would be perpendicular to the boat, while your rod's arc would be parallel to the water. This method can be an effective way to spread the lines out a little and make it easier to fish two or three lines from a small boat.

If you are using tube lures, they are best fished from the rod holders and the tube twisting imparts the action. Be aware of the twisting, especially if your backing is tied straight to your wire without a swivel; consider adding an extra swivel somewhere when using a tube to eliminate the twist from your line. If you are getting totally covered up with bluefish and you are hoping for a striper or two, as can often be the case at Sankaty, a tube can be effective. The hooks in the tube are only in the front and back, many bluefish will attack the middle and they will not get hooked. Stripers will try to swallow it whole and usually get either the front or rear hook. While you will probably hook a few blues who have the misfortune to grab it by the head or tail, hopefully their missed strikes will keep it in the water long enough for a few stripers to get a look at it.

Modern fish finders are extremely helpful when fishing Sankaty and the rest of the waters along the island's eastern shore. Anyone listening to the charter boat radio chatter will often hear, "Are you marking any?" which means, "Are you seeing any fish on the fish finder?" While fish at Sankaty do show themselves on the surface from time to time, for the most part, they are deep and the way to find them is to intently watch the fish finder for solid little blobs sitting tight to the bottom. Getting to know your fish finder will take some time, being able to make a good guess as to what is a striper and what is something else (bluefish, bait, etc.) will come with use as well as knowing where your lines are in relation to the little blips on your fish finder screen.

In times of frustration, when you know the fish are there, or you are looking at what you think is fish on your fish finder and not getting bites, lightening the leader can help. Dropping down to thirty or forty pound and switching from mono to fluorocarbon can help get bites.

Occasionally in fishing you will come across a situation where conventional wisdom and common sense must be disregarded. On one frustrating day I was trolling through what appeared to be fish with no bites, and fellow captain Brian Borgeson was next to me getting bites. He advised me to cut my leader off totally and twist my parachute straight to the wire. I was desperate enough to try this, and when we dropped it back out, the leaderless parachute was almost immediately eaten. It worked that day, and it has worked on a couple of occasions since, when the fish did not seem to want to eat, and I was desperate enough to try it again. I will not even venture a guess as to why it works, and I would certainly not advocate fishing leaderless parachutes on a regular basis, but sometimes desperation leads to innovation.

Personally, watching my fish finder intently and/or jigging a parachute on a heavy rod and wire line is not my ideal day of striper fishing. That being said, it is hard to argue with the results. If your main objective is to catch stripers, and how you catch them is only a secondary concern or perhaps not a concern at all, trolling Sankaty and the surrounding water with wire should be at or near the top of your list. It will consistently produce all season, and at times, especially in the middle of summer, it will be the only game in town.

Sankaty Without Wire-Line

While wire lining is certainly the most common and most effective way to fish Sankaty and the rest of the waters on the eastern shore of Nantucket, it is not the only way. Live bait is an option and unlike wire, you can scale down your tackle if you desire. Live eels are the most common bait of choice, both because of their effectiveness and availability. Currently, live eels are the only live bait available for purchase on the island. An eel is an extremely hardy bait, and keeping them alive takes very little effort. A live-well is not necessary, and unless you want to keep your eels for a number of days, it is an unnecessary difficulty. I have always had the best luck putting some damp seaweed and a plastic bag full of ice in a small bucket with a top (you can buy the bucket where you buy the eels but you are on your own for seaweed and ice). A lot of standing water is not necessary, but the top most certainly is, as eels are highly mobile in and out of water. If they are kept cold and damp, they will last for at least twenty-four hours. If you are fishing early before the tackle store opens, it is no problem to get the eels the afternoon before. The ice has the added benefit of making the eels lethargic, which makes them much easier to handle and hook, which is a difficult task. Using a cloth or towel to grab your cold eel makes it easier. Some people prefer to hook their eels through one jaw or both jaws, in through the mouth and out an eye, or through the tail. My preferred method is up from the bottom, through both jaws, and out, although I probably like that method only because it is the most aesthetically pleasing.

Live eels can be fished on spinning or conventional reels. At Sankaty, a sinker of a couple ounces or more will probably be necessary to keep your eel in close proximity to the bottom, which is where you want it. To use a sinker, either run your main line through an egg sinker or a fish finder rig (a small plastic tube for your main line to run through with a clip attached for a sinker) to a swivel, and then tie your leader to the swivel. Use a monofilament or fluorocarbon leader; four feet of fifty-pound test is a good starting point.

Drop your eel to the bottom and just drift along with the current, letting your eel do his thing. When using a spinning reel, keep the bail open and your finger on the line and when using a conventional reel keep the drag off and your thumb on the spool because once a fish hits it, it is necessary to give them slack and let them eat for some time. Keep in mind there is a lot of conflicting advice out there as to drop back times; years ago the standard advice was that you needed to let them eat for seven to ten seconds, but recently I have read several articles that advocate a very short drop back, and a few even recommend not fishing with an open bail or your drag off at all, and just dropping the tip when you feel a strike. Once you have given the fish time to eat (whatever that might be), engage the drag by flipping the bail or lever. If the line does not immediately come tight, reel until it does. If you are using a circle hook (which I highly recommend both for effectiveness and the health of the fish) the hook should become lodged in the corner of the fish's mouth and the fight will begin. If you are using a j-hook it may be necessary to set it once it becomes tight, but the hook is fairly likely to become lodged in the fish's stomach or gills after the necessary drop back. That will not only harm the fish but it will cause your leader to wear on the fish's jaws. Although stripers lack teeth their rough jaws are capable of significantly weakening and wearing through leaders.

Bluefish are an extreme nuisance if you are fishing with live eels. Quite often when you are striper fishing you are going to catch some bluefish. I try to look at them as a fun, hard fighting, high jumping gamefish. Maybe not the target species, but some welcome action nonetheless. When fishing live eels however, it is impossible to see them as anything but a huge irritation. Most often bluefish will come along, slice your eel to death for a bite or two and move on, and while eels are available for purchase, they are flown in and they are not cheap. Even if bluefish do bite the head and get the hook often times they will slice through your leader as well, liberating themselves quickly. Another advantage to using circle hooks is that you stand a better than average shot of hooking them in the corner of the mouth and catching the bluefish and getting your rig back instead of just a frayed mess of monofilament or fluorocarbon.

Another option for live bait is scup, also known as porgies. Live scup are quickly gaining popularity as a striper bait all over the Northeast, and Nantucket is no exception. Captain Mike Laufle of the *Double Take* started summering on Nantucket a couple years ago, and using his extensive Floridian knowledge of live baiting, he quickly became an island leader in catching striped bass on live scup. Laufle does most of his striper fishing at Sankety. In terms of rigging, he prefers long leaders of fifteen to twenty feet connected to the main line with a swivel. Above the swivel, he uses just enough weight to hold the bottom, usually about one ounce. At the end of the leader he uses 7/0 circle hooks and he takes the time to bridle the scup. For a quick and easy way to bridle a live bait, you will need a rubber band

and an open-eyed rigging needle. Secure the rubber band to the hook, then using the needle, thread the rubber band through the nose of the scup, then loop the rubber band back over the hook point. There are several good online videos that show this and many other bridling methods, and watching the process is certainly helpful. A bridled scup will live longer and swim more naturally than a scup that has the hook through it. Bridled baits will also result in more solid hook-ups because virtually the entire hook is exposed. Once the scup is bridled, Laufle deploys it to the bottom and fishes the rods from holders with the drag engaged. With the long leader, a dropback is not usually necessary, and with the boat drifting in the current, the rod holder does a nice job of setting the circle hooks. Laufle also enjoys considerable success on live eels using the same rigging and method, the only exception being he merely hooks the eels through the mouth rather than bridling them.

The Krill Show

In the last decade or so, fishermen in different parts of the Northeast have seen striped bass congregate to feed on krill. In my experience it has always happened in August off Sankaty and the eastern shore of the island, and it usually takes place a little further offshore in water a little deeper than the most typically productive spots.

Stripers eating krill is one of the coolest, most interesting things to see on the water, as well as one of the most supremely frustrating; picture thousands of fish, in schools ranging anywhere in size from that of a car to that of a football field, coming to the surface, packed together so tightly that they are actually rubbing and falling off each other's backs. They open and close their mouths as they slowly move along the top, gulping the krill.

The enormity of the schools is amazing, and to see them falling all over each other, gulping the surface is quite something. However, if you find stripers eating krill, catching one is probably going to be very difficult, and having literally thousands of fish feeding on the surface while your rod remains unbent can quickly wear on your sanity.

Trying to imitate krill, or "matching the hatch" as it is known in trout fishing, is difficult if not impossible. While some types of krill can grow to an inch or more, the krill that stripers feed on around Nantucket is very small; I would estimate that you could fit about ten or twenty of them on a dime. That makes any kind of single krill imitation impossible. The krill generally have a brownish-red hue and when the stripers are feeding on them they are usually thick enough to discolor the water. I have read about fly fisherman using krill flies, which are basically brownish-red blobs that are supposed to be mistaken for a little bunch of tightly packed krill. I have not tried it myself, but after witnessing how the fish feed on krill, I would say that laying a brownish-red blob in front of a feeding school would give you a pretty good shot at a bite.

I have thrown just about every lure in my tackle box at stripers eating krill, and none were especially effective. Occasionally, the fish would turn and eat the lure, and occasionally one would attack it upon landing seemingly out of frustration, but indifference and refusals are the far more common result. As usual, soft white plastics such as Hogys seem to be the most effective at drawing strikes on the surface, but they are far from effective.

While is often tough to focus your efforts sub-surface with thousands of fish burbling along the top, trolling wire-line around the schools is an effective way to get a few bites. The fish on the surface are so keyed into krill that any other offering is likely to be refused, but when stripers are visible feeding on krill on the surface, often times there are more fish below the surface, and the fish below the surface seem to be much more open to a different food item.

The fish spook fairly easily, and driving to close to a school, or having a school approach your boat only to realize at the last minute that you are there, will result in all the fish going down, in an amazing domino-effect of tail splashes, that in itself is a captivating thing to see. If you are fishing sub-surface, this isn't necessarily a bad thing. I will admit, that as a young and frustrated fisherman, a few times I put down the schools, or spooked them, on purpose where they would happily eat wire-lined parachutes. It was an effective method, but it felt wrong, and I am little embarrassed to divulge my actions. It seems that to me that when you are lucky enough to find stripers feeding on the surface, something I spend a good chunk of my life looking for, only bad karma can result from purposefully disturbing them and sending them scurrying to the depths.

If you find the krill show, perhaps the greatest piece of advice I can give you would be to put down your fishing rod and pick up a camera, because the sight is almost assuredly better than the fishing. After you have seen it, then go ahead and try a krill fly, or a Hogy or trolling on the outskirts.

Surface Feeding at Sankaty

Occasionally, especially in June and somewhat more sporadically in September, stripers will actively feed on the surface near Sankety. If baitfish are especially thick sometimes the stripers are coaxed off the bottom and chase the bait throughout the water column to the surface. If stripers are actively feeding on the surface at Sankaty, it will probably not be subtle. They will probably be accompanied by birds (seagulls, terns, and maybe a few others), and they will be boiling and splashing the water. In short, it is your typical surface feeding blitz.

The trick to getting bites in these situations is to be at the right place at the right time. It is rare that the fish will just stay put and continue to bust up the surface as you continually cast to them. More likely, the fish will be going down, popping up for a time when they find and corral a school of bait, and then go back down. When anticipating where the fish will pop up next, birds are your best friends. They will likely be over the bait and can lead you to the next surface blitz even before it starts. The run and gun method of seeing the fish and quickly running your boat within casting range is effective, but it may eventually put the fish down for good. If the fish are continually popping up in certain areas, drifting through the area is a more stealthy approach that may give you better shots at busting fish, as well as keep them busting longer.

In these active feeding situations, lure choice is not nearly as important as putting a lure in front of feeding fish, but sometimes even in the middle of what seems to be a feeding frenzy, stripers can be picky. Matching the hatch is the key to getting bites. At Sankaty (and most other places around Nantucket) this means sand eels. The skinny little minnows sometimes pass through in big clouds, and more often than not this is what the stripers will be after on the surface. A Hogy is my first choice. Yo-Zuri Crystal Minnows are also an excellent choice, and though they are much larger than a sand eel, they throw a lot of flash and seem to get noticed even in a crowd of natural bait. Pearl Bombers are another local favorite and an excellent choice, especially if the stripers are chasing slightly bigger baitfish or squid.

Heading down to Sankaty with a boat full of spinning rods, Hogys and plugs in search of some stripers is probably going to be disappointing. Usually the stripers at Sankaty stick close to bottom and their blitzes on the surface are unpredictable (a recent exception being late June of 2009 when stripers could be found feeding on the surface just about every slack tide for about two weeks). I would certainly recommend that when fishing Sankaty, have a spinning rod or two rigged and ready, keep an eye out for bird activity, and do not hesitate to investigate it.

Braided "Superlines" in Sankaty's Future

When you look at different striper fishing methods around the country, the twenty to thirty-five foot depths of Sankaty are certainly amongst the shallowest plied consistently with wire-line. I do not have answer for why that is, or why other methods of catching fish in this mid-range depth that work well in other areas do not produce like wire does at Sankaty. While forms of braided "super-lines" have been around for a while, within the past few years they have become more and more common in saltwater. Line diameters of only a fraction of similar strength Dacron and monofilament, and no stretch, make them ideal for different types of bottom fishing. Many types of bottom fish are being successfully targeted with butterfly and other jigs, that now, with the use of braided line, are able to be dropped with a degree of precision and given an appealing action, to depths far more than thirty-five feet. On my mental list of things to experiment with, fishing with some different artificials on braid while drifting at Sankaty has been near the top for couple years. Unfortunately, the vast majority of my time at Sankaty is spent with paying customers, and I do not think that is the appropriate time for playing around with something new. Captain Josh Eldridge of the *Monomoy* has had some success with artificials fished on braided line, and he is fine tuning them. One appealing aspect of this method, in his experience, is that it often yields a mixed bag of fluke, black sea bass and stripers. Hogy Lures now offers a variety of soft-plastics and rigging options intended to ply the depths. While certainly this type of fishing is in infancy in Nantucket, I personally look forward to doing some experimenting. I predict that within a few years fishing Sankaty with braided line and a variety of artificials will emerge as another productive wire-line alternative.

Eastern Rips

South and east of Nantucket exists a vast network of shoals, where water depths change rapidly from thirty feet or deeper to ten feet or shallower and then back down again in a very short area. Much like Great Point, the tide runs across these edges creating rips, and the rips hold fish.

A Very Lively Edge on the Rose & Crown
Notice the easily discernable first wave of the rip or "the edge,"
the bird activity, and the points and bowls of the edge
Photo courtesy of Chris Gorab Photography

The waters east of the island are influenced by the cold Labrador Current that comes south through the Gulf of Maine inshore of the warm-water Gulfstream. Hence, the water on these edges tends to stay cool throughout the summer, and when inshore water temperatures are in the seventies, and the stripers are not active or not there, you can still often find temperatures on these edges in the low sixties. There are hundreds of edges that hold fish and congregate bait. The fish are in the rip in order to eat, and when you find them, they usually bite. These edges offer some of the best, most consistent striper fishing anywhere in the world; catching ten stripers on one tide is on the slow side, and catching thirty is certainly possible.

The current problem with most of these rips is that they are beyond three miles offshore in federal waters, and you are not allowed to kill or retain striped bass from these waters, nor are you allowed to even "fish for striped bass." However, you are allowed to fish there.

I wrote to the National Marine Fisheries Service to ask for some clarification, and to specifically ask if catch and release fishing for striped bass more than three miles offshore was illegal. They were able to direct me to a single instance years ago of a charter boat captain off New Hampshire who was in an all striped bass tournament, who caught and released a striped bass beyond three miles offshore, entered the fish in the tournament, and was prosecuted civilly by the NMFS. He eventually settled the case. Beyond that, they were not able to direct me to another instance where somebody was prosecuted for fishing beyond three miles without killing or retaining stripers. Even the people in charge of the regulations do not really understand them because I specifically asked if it was legal to fish for bluefish, bonito and false albacore in the rips, and they were not able to answer me. That being the case, I do not encourage you to break the regulations, but if you happen to be fishing the Rose & Crown or the other outer rips "for bluefish" and releasing any stripers you catch, the authorities seem unable, or at least unwilling, to stop you.

Enforcement of the policy as a whole is between spotty and nonexistent. Most commercial and recreational anglers who break the regulations and kill fish beyond the three miles do so with impunity. It is disappointing because even if you are there trying to do the right thing, and release the fish, you cannot do anything about the guy next to you who is killing dozens of them, because your activities are also in a legal grey area.

While I do not advocate that you break the regulations, I do hope the policy is changed to something that makes sense. Right now the regulation hurts everybody: the anglers unable to access the great fishing, law enforcement that is in no way able or prepared to enforce the rules, and the fish that suffer from widespread poaching. Recreational anglers should be able to go and fish the spots, and I would like to see them be able to take one or two fish per boat for dinner. Regulations to ensure the majority of fish are released healthy and alive, such as the mandatory use of circle hooks, should also be adopted. This would benefit anglers, the local economy that suffers when striped bass are unavailable to visitors and locals, and the fish, because with anglers on the water there doing the right thing, most poaching would end.

In anticipation of the regulation being changed for the better, I will go through some of the spots and their approximate locations. I will also discuss how to fish them, and even with the current regulations this information will be useful because Quidnet Rip and most of the Old Man Shoal lie within three miles, and it is legal to fish for and take striped bass from them.

The Old Man Shoal is the southernmost shoal visited with frequency from anglers (Davis Shoal and Asia Rip lie beyond it to the south, but it is rare I hear of a trip there in search of stripers due to their distance from the island). As the southernmost shoal, influenced to some degree by the Gulfstream and less by the Labrador Current, the water temperatures are generally higher than the shoals farther to the east and north. It is the first rip to hold fish in the spring; some years it heats up by Memorial Day, and others not until mid-June. Usually by mid-July it is inundated with bluefish and getting a striper out of it is a difficult task. The Old Man is just south of Sankaty, and it is largely within three miles, so taking striped bass from all but the southern tip of it is legal.

As the summer moves on and water temperatures rise, the better fishing will shift north and east. The 6-Can Rip is an easily tolerable six mile jaunt east of Great Point. It starts just north of the Great Round Shoal Channel next to what is now the 8-Can bouy, but used to be the 6-Can, from which the spot got its name. Its edges rise to within five or six feet of the surface in a couple spots. There is a little bowl at the southern end of it, and then a series of little edges form as you head north, and it is all productive.

Just south and little east of the 6-Can is McBlair Shoal, which is a deeper edge than most, never rising closer than about fifteen feet from the surface.

The water temperature here can be downright cold, often running significantly cooler than the nearby 6-Can or the Rose & Crown Shoal just to the south. It was pretty slow in 2011, but it is a favorite of mine and while you will often run into a small crowd at the 6-Can, you will usually have McBlair to yourself.

A couple miles southeast of McBlair, and you will be at the Rose & Crown, the largest and most famous of the shoals. It covers several square miles and incorporates hundreds of edges. Depths in spots adjacent to it plunge to more than one hundred feet and for a big stretch toward its southern tip it rises to within about five feet of the surface. On most days getting anywhere near this shallow section is not advisable as huge breakers coming in from the Atlantic crash over it. Usually, the fishing gets good at the 6-Can, McBlair and the Rose & Crown a few weeks after the Old Man. Fishing tends to remain more consistent on the Rose & Crown throughout the summer, while the 6-Can and McBlair sometimes peter out a bit in mid-summer. Sometimes, however, the water on the Rose & Crown will heat up while the 6-Can, McBlair, and more distant Orion and 2-Can, (all situated further north) will stay a little cooler and have better fishing.

Unfortunately, the 6-Can, McBlair, and the Rose & Crown, all lie well outside the three-mile limit, making some of the best striped bass fishing in the entire world technically off limits for the time being.

The only option for fishing a deep rip other than the Old Man inside the three mile limit is Quidnet Rip, about two and half miles east of Sankaty. I have had some fantastic days there, especially in the fall, but it is hit or miss. Its most appealing feature is that it happens to be just inside the three-mile limit.

Much like fishing the rip at Great Point, the fish in the outer rips will primarily be feeding right on the edge, or a short distance in front of it or behind it. One of the best aspects of the offshore rips is that the fish can be found and caught at or near the top and light tackle can be utilized.

The edges east of the island vary from shoal to shoal but for the most part they rise to within ten or fifteen feet of the surface. As compared to Great Point, the increased depth makes sight fishing less likely (though it can still be very effective at times) but the cooler, deeper water makes the fish less finicky and more prone to eating; if the conditions are right, these rips produce some of the best striper action on earth.

As far as lures go, the standard starting point for all of Nantucket's captains for these rips is a large white swimming plug, such as a Pearl Bomber. I find myself using more and more big white soft plastics (Hogys) on the edges, and much like inshore, they seem to get more bites on tough days when the fish are a little more selective.

If the fish are not feeding on or near the surface, but you want to stay with light tackle, I have found success in the past bouncing a bucktail or a soft plastic with a weighted head along the bottom over the shoal's edge. It is not easy to do given the screaming tides you will find on the edges, but if you cast thirty yards or so in front of the edge, and let your lure sink to the bottom before retrieving it, with some trial and error you should be able to get your offering down and bouncing where the fish are. The same Sankaty wire-line setup with 150 feet of wire, a leader and a parachute jig with a pork rind is very effective on the edges. It will often produce a few fish when nothing else works. If you are trolling wire line, always try to have an idea of where your lure may be. If you are using light tackle you can effectively troll or cast keeping your boat within fifty feet of the edge, making it easy to see your lures and position them on or near the edge. With wire line it is a little more difficult because you have to let out more than 150 feet of line. You never want to fish with the wire-line in the guides because it may cause the wire to kink, especially when jigging. Make sure to let the entire section of wire out until only backing is left running through your entire rod. You will probably still want to focus on the edge, and you will have to estimate where your lure is. If you are just trolling down the edge fairly close to it, the tide is probably sweeping your lure through the edge and you are fishing way behind it. To keep you lure on the edge, your boat will need to be well out in front of it. When you hook a fish, and it comes to the surface quickly, get a good look at where it is, and try to get a sense of how far behind the boat it is, and this will help you judge the location of your lure more effectively. While close to the edge should always be your starting point, fishing wire back behind the edge can result in a few fish particularly on difficult days. For whatever reason, if the fish are not stacked up on the edge and you are not having any luck fishing the edge with light tackle or wire, the fish may be sitting behind the edge in the deep water, and a wire-line fished behind the edge may get them. Fishing wire line, both on the edge and behind it, can also be a good way to find a striper if the edge is seemingly full of bluefish.

I have also had a lot of success and a lot of fun fishing a Williamson's squid on the edges of the outer rips. They are large rubber squid that skip along the surface, much like the individual squid on a tuna spreader-bar. I skip it right on the first wave of the rip or right in front of it, and the stripers really throw themselves at it. I usually only use it on good days when arms are already tired from cranking, because due to their aggressive strikes, the hook-up rate is terrible, but it is certainly fun to watch. The fish with usually go fully airborne when attacking it, and watching the normally sub-surface stripers fly out of the water is worth a few missed bites (sometimes).

When using wire-line, obviously, you will be trolling, but with light tackle both trolling and casting can be effective. I generally start by trolling, keeping the Bombers or other offering within a few feet of either side of the edge, and casting if possible once a concentration of fish is located. Even when casting these rips, however, the boat will most likely be in gear and someone should be at the helm. The tide flies over the edges so quickly that if you were to position the boat in front on the edge and drift though, a very good caster would get two or maybe three casts with the lure passing through the productive zone before the tide would carry you out of range and you would need to reposition the boat. Having someone drive the boat, and stem the tide to keep you stationary, or moving slowly along the edge is important. When a fish is hooked, pulling them back through the rip on light tackle with the boat in gear will be difficult and will unnecessarily prolong the fight. Once a fish is hooked going into neutral and drifting through the edge or, if rough conditions dictate, driving out and turning the bow into the rip and then drifting once you get through the edge, will allow you to fight the fish more effectively.

While the rips east of the island play host to spectacular fishing and they are truly beautiful, they are no place for novice boaters. The tide rips across the edges at several knots and the depth changes quickly and dramatically. Even on seemingly placid days the wind, tide and rapid depth changes can create huge swells on the edges that come out of nowhere. Dangerous breakers cover parts of the shoals and even when Nantucket is clear, there is often thick fog over the cooler water east of the island that comes and goes without warning. Obviously, caution is necessary whenever you are on a boat, but the rips east of Nantucket can be particularly harrowing, and I would recommend that your first few trips be in the company of someone who has experience with them.

While the fishing can be spectacular, finding the fish can be somewhat daunting. If you are lucky enough to arrive at the Rose & Crown on a clear day with the tide running, just within your eyesight there may be a dozen good-looking edges, and fishing all of them will take more time than the tide will give you. On a great day, all the edges may be full of fish, but more often than not, the fish are bunched up in certain areas, and finding the little pockets of fish in amongst dozens of edges can be the difference between a slow day and an exceptional day.

The first step in narrowing down which edges to fish and which to bypass is to take a look around for a presence of life. Birds are the easiest to spot. Terns, seagulls, and a variety of other birds can sometimes be found working the edges, and they will most often lead you right to the fish. The birds will often work out in front of the edge and back behind the edge, while the good fishing, for the most part, will take place closer to the edge. Do not concern yourself with being right under the birds, just find the portion of the rip that the birds take an interest in, and fish that portion.

Bait is another key indicator of where the fish may be. Often times you will be able to spot bait showers in the edge and just in front of it. Most often, the bait on these edges is squid, but sand eels, little mackerel, and several other types of bait are possible. If bait is showering, something is harassing them from below and you should focus your efforts around the bait.

Under some circumstances, the fish themselves are visible. The fish can sometimes be seen surfing in the first wave of the rip, sitting almost motionless stemming the tide, or slowly sliding side to side waiting for a meal. If you have a tower, on the shallow edges, particularly on the west tide at the 6-Can, or a few places along the Rose & Crown, it is also possible at times to see them deeper in the water column, hanging around near the bottom. And finally, at times, the fish will be actively feeding on the surface making it impossible for you to miss them, pursuing bait with abandon, splashing around, and leaving the water completely at times.

In the best case scenario, you will arrive at an offshore rip to find everything happening, birds working, bait showering, and fish busting, but that is certainly not always the case. If you arrive at a rip and nothing visible is happening on or above the surface, do not fret. This varies widely from season to season, but arriving to a rip full of life visible on the surface is the exception rather than the rule, and yet good fishing is the rule, rather than the exception. Many, many times, I have fished rips and edges that look lifeless from the surface, and bites came quickly and regularly.

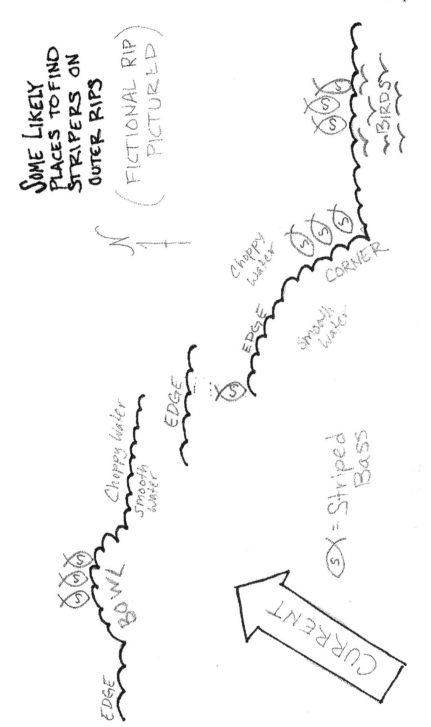

Some Likely Places to Find Stripers on Outer Rips

(Fictional Rip Pictured)

= Striped Bass

CURRENT

If you arrive at an edge or series of edges that offer no signs on life on the surface, start looking in the areas where the edge changes. The contours of the shoals that form the rips have natural variations, and the edge is shaped by them. Corners, bends, and little bowls are formed in the edges, and all of them are good places to look for a concentration of fish. While it is certainly possible that a fairly straight and uniform edge is holding fish along it, it is more often the case the fish will be stacked up on the corners, turns, and indentations, and the uniform sections of the edge will not be as productive. These natural idiosyncrasies in the rips may concentrate bait, they may produce current fluctuations that make it easier to the stripers to stay put against the tide, and they may create a better ambush point than a straight edge, but in any case, they usually concentrate fish.

The sandbars that form the rips are somewhat fluid, and from season to season you may see changes in the edges, and changes in the best spots, but certainly, fishing where you found fish before is a good start. If you get a few bites in a little area, be sure to put it in your GPS, because even if you follow all of the above advice, you may find that your productive little spot looks just about the same as half a dozen other spots within sight that may or may not be holding fish.

Fishing the outer rips is exciting. Even in the height of summer, in the middle of the day, on light tackle, the fishing is usually still excellent. For the time being, you can get a taste of the action in the spring or the fall at the Old Man or Quidnet, and while I do not endorse it, if you want to go bluefishing at the Rose & Crown, you will likely find yourself releasing a lot of big beautiful stripers. What I certainly do endorse is you contacting your federal representative to see about getting the regulation changed to something that makes sense. Some of the best striper fishing in the world should not be off-limits and attractive to poachers, it should be protected with sound regulations as well as utilized and enjoyed by the fishing public.

FALL STRIPERS

In the hearts and minds of many anglers, all striped bass fishing prior to September is a mere prelude. Fall is when big fish in large groups are feeding round the clock with abandon, in preparation for and during their trip south. The fall migration is the stuff of legend, and in the literature of striper fishing, it is highly celebrated. Unfortunately, it seems to me that the actual fall striper run of late has fallen well short of the high expectations that fisherman place on it. I am not alone in this feeling, and many anglers, on Nantucket, Cape Cod, and further afield have been disappointed with the fall run. That sounds like a lot of doom and gloom, and it is not wholly unwarranted given the lack of sound conservation measures and general population decline of the last several years. Nevertheless, there is plenty of good fishing to be had in the fall, and certainly, if management practices improve, we can look forward to some legendary fall blitzes again.

Of all the striper seasons, I am least familiar with fall. During high school, like most Nantucket boys, I put down my rod and picked up football pads for the fall, and Whaler football, being what it was and is, left little room for other pursuits. After high school, I was home from college by mid-May in plenty of time for the best that spring had to offer, but I was headed off-island again in late August well before any kind of fall fishing heated up. Only in the last few years have I been around to experience the fall, and though I have fished it fairly hard, I have to admit that it is not with the same zeal and single-minded devotion with which I approach springtime stripers. Not that I tire of fishing, but it is a little easier to get distracted when you have fished about ninety-four of the past one hundred days, as is likely my story come September. Another reason for this is that unlike in June, striped bass have some competition for attention. In 2011,

I fished the hardest of any fall of my life, but there was a lingering bonito bite and a red-hot false albacore bite, and most of my time was spent targeting them.

Fall fishing is like spring fishing, only, in my experience, less predictable. Every spot and every method mentioned previously has the potential to really heat up in the fall. Fish that moved out of the harbor in the height of summer return when the water cools to take advantage of the copious forage. When flats fishing was first getting popular, September was often named with June as a top time to target them, and while it has been my experience that their numbers are not what they are in the spring, there is absolutely no doubt that some fish return to the shallows as early as late August, and through September you can expect some good shots at fish. Great Point often heats up in spurts during the fall, usually with the stripers in amongst the bluefish that time of year, and usually just about as happy to inhale your offering. Sankaty can be excellent in the fall, and if the fish are there they are often a little more active and aggressive, and the precision necessary in the height of summer can be replaced by simply putting your lure in the water.

As for the deep-water rips, fall is a great time, especially since those within the three-mile limit, Quidnet Rip and most of the Old Man Shoal, often fill with stripers again. Quidnet is a funny, fickle little rip that may or may not hold fish at any point during the year, but September and October are when you are most likely to find a lively, active rip full of stripers. In July and August the Old Man is usually packed with bluefish shoulder to shoulder, and even if there are a few stripers lying below it is difficult to get a lure by the bluefish. In September and October, often the ratio becomes a little more favorable for striper hopes, and the Old Man can yield some great mixed bag days on wire-line and sometimes spinning gear.

While the fall run may not have materialized into the epic proportions that many expect from it in recent years, it is still a very good time for striper fishing. While fishing in October, the fact that very soon my next fishing is either several months or a plane ride away is never far from my thoughts, and spending some bundled-up October days on the water always seems like a fitting way to wind the season down.

"Traditional" Surf Fishing

The only method and locations I have left to place under the heading of fall is what I will refer to as "traditional" surf fishing. Much like fly fishing, it is romantic and it inspires a lot of writing, both instructional and contemplative in nature. There is a contingent of anglers who strongly prefer having terra firma underfoot than the deck of boat; striped bass are their fish. Nowhere in the angling world is the surf contingent more represented than East Coast striper fishing. Stripers' home waters abut the populous eastern seaboard, and their preference for spending a big chunk of their lives within a cast's length from shore makes them consistently accessible to droves of surf fisherman. Surf fishing for stripers has a long and storied history, much like fishing the fall run itself. It is in homage to the old school, to the traditional yet still highly effective methods of pursuing stripers from big-water shorelines, that I have placed surf fishing in the fall, rather than the recently more consistent spring.

What I mean by "traditional" surf fishing is fishing big water, usually with fairly stout tackle. This is not a definition or usage that is common; I have invented the distinction here only in an attempt at organization. I am not only talking about Nantucket's South Shore, with its roaring surf; I also include Great Point, Smith's Point, Eel Point, the east and most of the north shore. However, I do not mean any type of fishing that is done without a boat. For instance, in terms of tackle and methods, and even location, I would classify walking and wading the shores of Madaket Harbor as flats fishing rather than surf fishing. Obviously, these lines are imaginary and even there they are not clear, but it is really nothing to be concerned about because I do not see how a clear line would help you catch more fish, and whether you caught your striper while wading the flats or plying the surf, the important part is that you caught a striper.

It is obvious that I am not among the pure surf contingent, the bulk of my fishing these days being from a boat. Despite the fact that after the first few weeks of fishing, I do not usually put in a lot of time on the South Shore and other traditional surf casting spots these days, preferring the flats and the harbors, it would be totally negligent to not include these spots beyond the early May search for schoolies. Even if you are not among those under the spell of surf fishing, it is hard to argue with its convenience, and on Nantucket it is especially convenient. If you have an hour to kill, you can drive straight until you hit water, hop out and take a few casts, and have some hope of success. Unless you are inclined to believe that just by taking a few casts you are already, on some level, successful- a mindset I wholeheartedly endorse.

This is nothing more than a guess, but given that there is no way to be proven wrong, I would say that the South Shore from Smith's Point around to Sankaty accounts for the majority of Nantucket stripers taken from the beach. That is really not going out on much of limb since I just named a huge chunk of productive water, but I would guess that beach anglers along this shore take more fish than all my beloved harbor spots (both town and Madaket), the north shore, and Great Point combined.

With that said, the entire shoreline is worth consideration, and despite the geographic distinctions, each can be approached in a similar way, with the exception being the shallow water north and east of Eel Point (which are flats and are best approached with the flats tactics already discussed). The South Shore, running from Smith's Point to Sankaty, is the open Atlantic and the surf coming ashore is the island's biggest. The rate of the drop-off varies widely from place to place, but even where it is shallow, wading any distance offshore is not advisable due to the high surf and strong currents. The island's shoreline turns and heads north around Siasconset and extends to Great Point. While the eastern shore of the island is still the open Atlantic, the large network of shoals to the east knocks down the swells before they reach land. The eastern shore drops off fairly quickly, and the currents can still be treacherous. The swells, though not the surfable rollers of the South Shore, are sometimes deceptively big and powerful. The north shore of the island, from Great Point, down to Coatue, skipping across the mouth of the harbor and extending to Eel Point, is the Nantucket Sound side. It is placid compared to the raw power of the South Shore and the deceptive currents of the eastern shore, and much of the area is conducive to wading.

While I do not haunt the South Shore into the summer much anymore, I certainly have put in some time there over the years. In my high school days my rod of choice was a ten footer, a little on the short side for a surf rod perhaps, but it was versatile, and it got plenty of use. A night I spent at Nobadeer over Memorial Day weekend with my aforementioned Uncle Bob, a friend of his, and my brother, is one of my most memorable striper trips ever. We were casting the local favorite, big Pearl Bombers, and as the sun went down, big stripers started feeding. Rather than coming in tight to the shore, the fish were staying fairly far out, beyond the breakers. Luckily, we were all trained on surf fishing for blues, where throwing your plug a country mile was often a requirement for success. We had a handful of Bombers we had filled with water on the advice of my father, who claimed that was what the guys in the know did back in his youth. We would chuck the water-filled bombers as far as we could, well beyond the breakers, and even then if you didn't get a bite within your first fifteen cranks or so, you wouldn't get one at all. The fish were uniformly the biggest I had encountered up until that time, all solidly into mid-thirty inch range with a couple approaching forty. The ferocious bites were just the beginning with big runs and stubborn fights following. Getting those big fish in through the surf was no easy task, but our ratio was good enough that I remember catching a lot of fish that night rather than losing a lot.

When surf fishing, I recommend using a rod that is long and fairly stout. Eleven feet is a good starting point, and although a fourteen-foot monster is pretty cool, you probably are not going to miss out on too many fish if your rod is only eight or nine feet. Many of your lures (especially if you want to be able to take advantage of bluefish with the same rod) are going to weigh several ounces so you need a rod stout enough to handle those.

Lipped swimming plugs, such as the oft-mentioned Pearl Bomber, are a good starting point. Filling them with water does add some weight, although it can make them swim a little funny. If you are inclined to fill them with water, just heat a thin piece of metal, a paper clip works well, and once it is good and hot, stick it through the back of the lure into the hollow middle. You can fill them with a hypodermic needle, but, thankfully I suppose, my brother and I did not have easy access to hypodermic needles during our childhood, and we figured out how to do it fairly easily without one. First, fill your mouth with water, and then place your lips on the lure and create a seal around the hole. Bend your neck forward so the lure is under your mouth and the water in your mouth is covering the hole in the lure. Suck some air out of the lure creating a vacuum, and water from your mouth will rush into the lure to replace the air you have sucked out. Repeat the suction process several times until you are satisfied with the amount of water in the lure. Keep your lure upright and dry it off. Reheat your piece of metal and use it to smush a little melty plastic back over the hole, and you are all done. If you want to skip the water, several manufacturers are now offering heavier swimming plugs with things like "weight transfer balls" designed to cast greater lengths, but experience has taught me that fish love the Pearl Bomber, and the new-fangled ones may or may not work as well.

Large metal lures, such as the Hopkins, Deadly Dick, and Kastmaster are also effective in the surf, and if you are facing a stiff wind that a swimming plug can't get through, a metal spoon is a great option. Soft plastics, both tails on jig heads, Hogys rigged with a weight, and fully-cast plastics like Storm Minnows are all good choices. Surf fisherman especially seem to be very fond of teasers, that consist of a streamer fly attached to line above lure, either by way of a dropper loop or a three-way swivel. In addition to just having another hook in the water and giving the fish another option, most proponents of the teaser rig argue that it represents a small fish (the fly) being chased by a larger fish (the plug), and this imitation of the food chain in action really excites stripers.

Live eels are a good option when surf fishing. I would recommend using the same technique discussed in fishing them along the west jetty. Cast them out and retrieve them very slowly, and effectuating a drop back by dropping your tip and if possible taking couple steps toward the fish.

Fishing dead bait for stripers is not a terribly common practice on the island, and within my lifetime, it has never been. In other parts of the stripers' range, fishing dead bait is quite common, and I am at a loss to explain why it is not practiced more often on Nantucket. I do not know anyone who does it with regularity, but I think it may be expanding in popularity. Local tackle shops are selling more frozen mackerel than ever and it is not as uncommon as it was a few years ago to see a guy watching a rod in a sand-spike. I once caught a nice striper on an entire squid that I dropped in the hole off Second Point after I ran out of eels, and that is the entirety of my dead bait experience, but that will not prevent me from offering some of my thoughts. While stripers can be extremely picky, they eat a huge variety of different things, and their sense of smell is excellent and can lead them right to dead bait. After big storms where sea clams are battered out of their shells, stripers take advantage of it and feast on the clams, and in-turn anglers take advantage of that. I would not be surprised if soaking a clam on the South Shore after a big storm was productive. I will not get into specific rigs, methods and varietals of baits, leaving that to somebody who actually has some experience, but if you want to soak some bait for stripers, I say, why not? More power to you, and good luck.

I will not go into too much detail regarding how to "read the surf" and determine from the shape of waves and the shoreline where the fish may be hiding, there is plenty of good literature out there dealing specifically with reading the surf, but I will offer a little guidance. First, and most obviously, keep an eye out for fish, and secondly, birds. Constantly be looking around and scanning the water for fish breaking or swirling, or for birds diving. Next, much like finding fish in a rip, any change, or difference, or out of place feature, may hold fish and is worth some casts. For example, if the shoreline is fairly straight, but a small point juts out, focus your efforts around the point rather than the featureless shoreline. Perhaps even more important than the shoreline, are the characteristics of the water. If the waves are breaking uniformly along the beach, except for one spot where they seem to break with less force or they do not break at all, fish that spot thoroughly. Waves break when it becomes too shallow for them to sustain themselves, and if the waves are not breaking in a certain spot, that means the water there is deeper than the surrounding water in which the waves are breaking. Stripers will often sit in these little troughs, avoiding some of the turbidity of the breakers. Conversely, if any area is especially rough compared to the surrounding water, give it some casts too. The roughness could be caused by the spot being shallow or by a current pushing against the waves. In either case, the stripers probably are not sitting right in that water but they may be on the edges of it actively racing into to feed whenever a baitfish (or your lure) gets caught in it and makes itself an easy target. No matter what the difference is, differences are good and they attract fish.

As I mentioned when targeting the first arrivals of the year, and contrary to my good night at Nobadeer, the fish are often tight to the beach. Fish like changes, and there is no bigger change than ocean to land. Often casting out at an angle and retrieving your lure somewhat parallel to the beach rather than consistently perpendicular to it will yield better results.

As you move from the first arrivals into the bigger fish and from early May into June, and into the height of summer, hitting the beaches at sunset and sunrise will begin to be more productive and more important. For those of you inclined toward night fishing, the wee hours can be great.

Stripers venture closer to shore and become more active as the sun goes down, and often do the bulk of their feeding at night.

Sorting out fishing reports and rumors can be a nightmare. Luckily I am on the water daily, and in the confidences of enough guys who are also on the water daily, so most of the information I get is usually very current and more or less reliable. If you are not on the water everyday, and you do not have a trusted network of friends and confidants, getting a decent report is a difficult task. The guy at the tackle store may be inclined to tell you that big fish are biting everywhere, the guy that went fishing two weeks or twenty-five years ago is more than happy to fill you in on the details of his triumphs, real or imagined, and even if you are lucky enough to come across somebody who actually crushed them last night, giving you the full scoop may not be their utmost priority. That being said, if you are going to try to locate some good surf fishing, it is probably worth your time to wade into that pool of nonsense and try to come away with whatever good and current information you can. If you are going to be surf fishing on a regular basis (or any kind of fishing for that matter), building your network of confidants is very important. When you share good information with the right people, they will probably repay the favor when they are able. Shore bites often happen for a few nights, or mornings, or more rarely, days, at a time. While certainly surf-fishing can be a here today, gone tomorrow type of thing, it is just as likely, for instance, that whatever set of circumstances came together to produce good fishing at Cisco one night will commence again the next night (perhaps an hour later adjusting for tide).

If you are unable to get what you determine to be a good fishing report, or even a bad one, I will give you a few spots, but I do not advise you to put a lot of faith in these spots. Recalling my good Memorial Day at Nobadeer and going there with expectations of big stripers grabbing every third or fourth cast is probably going to end in disappointment. On the other hand, you are assuredly not going to catch any fish by staying on your couch, and if you don't have a better idea, go fish Nobadeer and hope for big stripers.

I have always liked to start pretty much right at the end of the runway of Nantucket Airport, and move in whichever direction looks promising from there. I have had success at Miacomet, not just with schoolies, but also as the season wears on. In the summer of 2011, I heard more reports of fish being caught at Cisco than any other beach. Not a summer goes by without some great nights on Low Beach and Sankaty. I used to frequent Eel Point, and while this may have been the first step toward my evolution into a harbor and flats guy, at first I always fished the deep water in the channel off the point with a traditional surf rod and big plugs and did fairly well. In that particular spot I always enjoyed the best action on the outgoing tide.

My last piece of advice in regards to surf fishing, is to keep it moving. Stop and linger around the features that may hold fish, but I would only give the best of them eight or ten unproductive casts before moving on. Until you find some fish, there is really no reason to stop. I like to walk down the beach, fishing as I go, or sometimes, drive down the beach, stopping where it looks fishy. While the fish may be moving around and may find you even if you are standing still, you are just as likely to encounter them if you are moving around too, and if the fish are not moving, you certainly are not going to encounter them standing still.

CHAPTER TWO

Bluefish

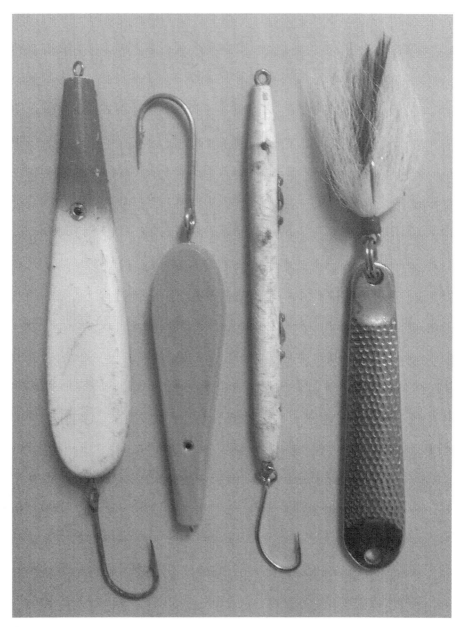

Nantucket Bluefish Essentials

Left to Right: Red Headed Ballistic Missile (2 3/8 oz.) complete with teeth marks, Orange Ballistic Missile (1 ½ oz.), used and abused Spofford's Needlefish, Hopkins

If I were to set out to design the perfect gamefish, I would want a fish that pulls hard, jumps often, has a never-say-die attitude. It would exhibit enthusiasm for topwater lures, be consistently hungry and aggressive, and could usually be found. As you already know or could guess, I have just described the bluefish. To be honest, my perfect gamefish would also be more prone to a long and fast first run, and maybe be a little bigger and a little prettier, but the bluefish still fits the criteria best than most.

Despite possessing many of the qualities anglers profess to like in fish, bluefish remain a much-maligned species, especially since striped bass populations rebounded and we ceased to "Think Bluefish." I am among the guilty too, often more irritated than excited when I see a bluefish leap skyward with my lure in his mouth. I have arrived at rips, upset to find fish shoulder to shoulder and jumping out of the water because they were blues. I have preached the virtues of bluefish one minute, and cursed them the next. There are certain times when bluefish are going to be source of aggravation, especially when they savagely render delicate or expensive offerings useless at an alarming rate. Even a bluefish aficionado is probably not going to smile upon them when they slice a dozen pricey eels to ribbons, reduce a bag of Hogys to a bunch of bit-off stubs, or slice off a half dozen Yo-Zuris meant for bonito at fourteen bucks apiece. In my own re-education on the virtues of bluefish, I think the key lies in targeting them. If you make bluefish your target, rather than an incidental catch, your tackle will be matched to them and each strike, pull and jump will cease to be an aggravation, and they can be an absolute pleasure.

I think a disdain for bluefish, while perhaps trendy right now in the fishing world, is not going to do you any good and it probably going to cause you to miss out on some great fishing. I will share a couple stories to help you either curb your disdain or stave it off, or perhaps if you are already enlightened, just to keep you loving bluefish.

One afternoon in the spring I was motoring out of Hither Creek in a skiff, and Doug Lindley was returning in his boat. I was planning on fishing the flats for stripers. We each slowed to chat for a little while, and I asked him how the fishing was. Now, for those who do not know Doug, he is high on the short list I spoke of in the introduction. When I was a little kid, going downtown to see the fish weighed in the annual billfish tournament was something locals did. At the time, Doug was running a big sportfisher that was consistently at or near the top of the leader board. I remember watching him weigh a couple big blue marlin and impressive yellowfin tuna, and it made quite an impression. Doug has run boats and caught fish all over the world. He was a trailblazer in sight fishing white marlin south of the island, and I am told he pretty much invented live baiting them with scup. These days he is inshore more than offshore, and excels there too. He is also one of the few honest fishermen I know, if he tells you he caught ten, he caught ten. If you are under the impression you have seen more or caught more than Doug, and your last name is not Kreh or Murray, you are probably sorely mistaken.

Anyway, as we slowed, Doug pointed out to the channel off Eel Point where some terns were working, and he said with a big smile, "There are plenty of bluefish out there under those terns." Here is guy who has fished the full moons of Saint Thomas, marlin fished Panama, sailfished Costa Rica, pioneered the canyons of the Northeast, and of late has taken a strong liking to bonito and false albacore on the fly, but bluefish working under terns provided him with a few hours of fishing bliss and a big smile.

When I left the dock I had no intention of targeting bluefish, and at first I didn't know what to think of this world-class captain and angler telling me he had just enjoyed some action with three-pound blues under the birds. After some thought it occurred to me that Doug has attained some level of fishing enlightenment several circles above most, where a hungry three-pound bluefish can produce as much joy and fulfillment as an angler needs.

The next occasion came in September. Mike Schuster and I were signed up for the *Inshore Classic*, a month-long tournament on the island, and we wanted to weigh in fly rod bluefish. We had caught some big bluefish at Great Point with clients for a couple days prior, and when a break in our charter schedule allowed, we loaded the fly rods and headed to Great Point. We arrived and started casting, and before long we each had a little bluefish. We stayed for a few hours, catching lots of little bluefish, hooking and routinely losing the big ones, and really having a fantastic time. The action was the sort of quality, consistent action that you can expect from bluefish under good circumstances, but it was not red hot. Perhaps most importantly, the fishing did not strike either of us as easy. The big ones were particularly difficult, and we left without a big fish to weigh, feeling like the score ended up with the bluefish on top. Especially when fly fishing, I would suspect that anyone who claims catching bluefish is "too easy" is very short on actual experience. On the way home, after a little thought, we both said how it had been a really good time, and wondered why we didn't do it more often.

I think what made that trip enjoyable was that bluefish were the target, rather than just an incidental catch when trying to for stripers, bonito or false albacore. While I do not anticipate abandoning the other species, or even reordering my preference in targeting them, I am going to consider more trips targeting bluefish in the future.

Springtime Bluefish

Bluefish arrive on Nantucket at some point in May, anywhere from a few days to a few weeks behind the striped bass. Sometimes they arrive in early May, and sometimes anglers in the *Hooked on Nantucket Memorial Day Bluefish Tournament* are looking for the first arrivals. The best way to anticipate their arrival, like with stripers is to follow fishing reports from the Vineyard. Unlike striped bass, however, the first bluefish of the year are usually found along the North shore. Off Dionis and Coatue are the best spots to find the first fish, and they continue to be the best places to fish for them for much of the spring.

In the spring, bluefishing is often about finding fish in open water. While Great Point and other rips are excellent places to find fish, the fish in the spring are very active chasing bait and moving around, and sometimes they do not settle into the rips to feed for quite some time. In addition to being the best place to find them in the spring, Bluefish are found in open water throughout the entire summer and fall, and along all of Nantucket's shores. They can be found in five to ten feet of water off Dionis and Coatue, in twenty to forty feet of water south and east of the island, and in the fifty to sixty foot depths in the Chord of the Bay. Blues can also be found on the flats and in the harbor, but I would not recommend them as spots to include in your search. While finding fish in open water is often the key to good springtime bluefishing, it is applicable for the entire season whether fishing from a boat or the beach, and the methods for finding them remain the same.

The key to finding fish in open water is to keep your eyes out. First, scan the horizon for birds. Sometimes, very large groups of feeding fish move through in the spring, and hundreds of birds join the action. If this is the case, it should be visible from miles around. The best situation is a mix of terns and seagulls actively hitting the water, but even just a few terns diving is worth some investigation. A few seagulls sitting around is probably nothing, but if a bunch of them are sitting around, they may be at the sight of a recent bluefish blitz waiting for the next one.

Next, keep your eyes peeled for "slicks." One of the best ways to find bluefish is to look for their slicks. Bluefish create an oily sheen on the water, making it a little slicker than the surrounding water. To give you an idea of what you are looking for, picture a beachgoer with some freshly applied sunblock who takes a swim, they create a pretty good slick too. When I was growing up, it was commonly said that bluefish are an oily fish, and oils from the bluefish themselves made the slicks. While blues may release some oils, I believe the creation of slicks to be primarily caused by feeding. Unlike the toothless striped bass, bluefish have a full complement of razor sharp teeth on both jaws. When they feed, they slice stuff to shreds, and a lot of pieces of bait are not immediately ingested. The blood and oils of all those shredded baitfish are released when the blues feed, and they float to the surface and create the slick. Bluefish are also known to continue feeding even when their stomachs are totally full, vomiting as they go, adding even more blood, oil and fish juice to the slick.

There are many other causes of slicks, and deciphering a bluefish slick from something else without wasting valuable fishing time on each one is key. Variations in the wind, tide and current also create slicks. Patches of water will naturally be a little calmer than other patches. The slicks caused by the wind are tide will probably be long and skinny, whereas bluefish slicks tend to be round, and while the surface of the water in a wind and tide slick will be slightly calmer than the surrounding water, it will often lack the metallic sheen of a bluefish slick. Certainly do not rule out slicks adjacent to the beach, bluefish often corral bait right along the beach and will feed tight to it, but beware of them. If someone fillets a fish on the beach and drops the fish carcass back in the water, a slick will form. If someone eating a sandwich and tosses the crust with a little mayonnaise on it into the water, a slick will form, and if the previously mentioned sunblocked bather takes a dip, you will see a doozy of a slick. It does not take very much oil at all to make a convincing slick. In a best case scenario, you will find a shiny round slick, or a couple of them, and more will keep materializing around you as bluefish find more bait and slice through it.

It is both obvious and often overlooked when searching for bluefish, but also scan the water nearest you for fish. Often times anglers are busy concentrating on locating birds on the horizon, or slicks in the distance that they drive right over bluefish that are just cruising along. While feeding bluefish will often draw a crowd of birds or create slicks, bluefish just cruising the surface are very common, and while they are a little more subtle than a flock of squawking birds or big silver slick, it is still fairly easy to see them. The first thing to look for, especially when running, is swirls. As your boat approaches the bluefish along the surface will dive, leaving a swirl or a few swirls in your path. When leaving the jetties and heading to Great Point, and again from Great Point south to Sankaty, you stand a pretty good chance of finding a few on the surface for the entire season. If you run over a few, do not worry. Just stop your boat, start looking around, and start casting. It is rare that you will find only one little group of fish on the surface. Usually, if you run over some fish there will be more little packs of them hanging around on the surface in close proximity.

The next thing to watch out for is tails. Bluefish will often tail in deep water. For those of you familiar with bonefishing, it is a very similar sight, except that while a bonefish will tail when the water is too shallow to contain them, bluefish tend to stick up their tails in deep water. They like to travel right on the surface at times, with their bodies angled down to keep an eye out for food, thrusting their tails into the air. Off Sankaty, off the south shore and in the deep water north of Coatue in Chord of the Bay, keeping an eye out for tails is a great way to spot fish. A bluefish tail out of the water is just a pointy little triangle. They are small and not particularly obvious, but once you get the hang of spotting them they become pretty clear. Unlike bonefish and other tailing species of the flats, you will not encounter any single fish. If one fish is tailing, quite few will be tailing making them much easier to spot and catch.

The fish themselves will also be visible at times, just under the surface of the water. Off Dionis and Coatue, in five to ten feet of water the bottom is generally sandy and you may be able to see them standing out against the bottom, and if you have the benefit of a tower or any kind of elevated vantage point that will help. Polarized glasses are an important tool for virtually any kind of fishing, but they are essential if trying to spot fish below the surface.

Another thing that can aid you in your search for bluefish is smell. Not always, but certainly sometimes, when there are bluefish in the area you will get the scent of fresh watermelon. I believe it has to do with the same feeding practices that create slicks, and the blood and oils being released by severed baitfish smell of fresh watermelon. It is usually just of subtle hint of watermelon, but it is there nevertheless. Sometimes it can lead to good fishing on its own, you will be driving along, smell some watermelon, and stop and catch fish where you wouldn't have stopped otherwise. Other times it can help you identify slicks as definitely bluefish. Oftentimes it will be after the fact, you will already have found the fish and be catching them and get a distinct nose full of watermelon. Other times you will be neck deep in bluefish all day and never get a whiff of any kind of fruit.

Trolling for blues is the standard method of the downtown charter boats, and it is a very effective way to catch fish, especially in rips, but it can also be a very effective way to locate fish even for those who prefer to cast and retrieve. If your visual search turns up no birds, slicks or fish, consider trolling. Just because you may not be equipped with big conventional reels and orange hoochies, don't be afraid to toss a few lines behind the boat and ride through some usual spots. Ballistic Missiles work very well when trolled, and you can adjust your speed to keep them skipping just right. It is hard to beat the hoochie for subsurface appeal, and it may pay to keep a couple in your box even if you are just going to attach them temporarily to a spinning rod. If you are driving around looking for fish indicators, a few lures behind your boat are often the most effective indicators. You can cover a lot of water effectively by trolling, and you are going to locate some fish that would not have been visible to you, but are there and hungry just the same. The fish may be travelling or hanging out five or ten feet below the surface, not feeding actively to create a slick or attract birds and too deep to be spotted, but nevertheless will happily rise to a trolled offering. Once you locate the fish, you can usually stop and cast productively.

While being able to find bluefish in big, largely featureless, open water is often the ticket in the Spring, there are some usual bluefish haunts to start your search. The first being the previously mentioned sandbars off Dionis and Coatue. Often the very first fish of the year, as well as the first consistent fishing, takes place in the sandy and patchy bottom in five to fifteen feet of water off the north shore beaches.

If nothing is to be had there, the deeper waters of Nantucket Sound, especially from the jetties east to Great Point, are a good next bet. I just named a huge chunk of water, and there is really no good way to narrow it down further so locating the fish in open water is important.

The waters of Nantucket Sound generally play host to good bluefishing before the southern and eastern shores. Sometimes bulk of the fish will remain in the sound for a few weeks, but other years the south and east shores will heat up only days after the bluefish arrive.

Spofford's Ballistic Missile is my favorite bluefish lure, and I do not have a close second. The sleek popper, designed to ride over the surface of the water skipping and splashing along it, is not totally unique in design. My preference for the Ballistic Missile is largely habit, and Roberts and other companies make similar plugs that are very effective. For color choice I like the red-head white body and the solid orange. On a day-to-day basis I do not like the green, but I always have a couple in my box. There are odd days when the bluefish do not exhibit their usual aggressiveness and it is tough to get them to bite. Green Ballistic Missiles have been the answer to this often enough in the past that I always try to have a couple with me.

To fish these lures, you generally want to cast as far as you are able. Even if you spot a fish, do not put the lure right on its nose, try to throw the lure well past the fish and retrieve it in front of the fish. The lures are dense and they sink fairly quickly, so you need to reel them fast enough to keep them skipping and bouncing along the surface. Under the water a Ballistic Missile does not look like a baitfish, it looks like a piece of plastic, and while bluefish are not known for their selectiveness, you are not going to get bites on a slowly retrieved Ballistic Missile. Cast, keep your rod tip up, and reel just about as fast as you can. Start your retrieve as soon as your lures spashes down, because if you let it sink at all, it will take a little while to get back to skipping along the surface. The skipping and splashing will attract bluefish and watching them come for it is exciting. They will usually pursue it with abandon, boiling on it, jumping out after it, chomping at everything. If a bluefish strikes your lure but misses it, my advice to beginners is to just keep reeling fast. A blue will usually come back and back and back until he either hooks himself or you get the lure back to the boat. Often times a few of his friends will join in the pursuit and they will take turns whacking your plug. If you stop your retrieve, which you may be your first instinct or perhaps even just a surprised reaction to the voracity of the strike, blues will quickly lose interest in your lure. Once you get the hang of it, is possible to increase your hook-up rate with just a slight deceleration in your retrieve. Sometimes after a few strikes, when I know there is one or more excited fish behind the lure, I will slow my retrieve just for a moment to give them a little easier shot at it. If it is not immediately successful, I immediately quicken my retrieve again, to ensure they do not lose interest. The timing of it is a little tricky to master, and slowing your retrieve down is playing with fire, but it certainly can be effective.

Most of the time, when you find the fish they are plentiful enough and aggressive enough that their repeated swings and misses at your lure are an extremely fun and visual part of the fishing. You would not want to hook one every time if you could, preferring to watch ten bites for every one hooked and still spending the majority of your time with your rod doubled-over in battle. However, there certainly are days when there are not enough fish or enough bites to make the misses fun, and sometimes even when there are plenty of fish the bites are all misses and you want a hook-up. Hook-up rates while beach fishing are even more of concern because you never know when the bluefish will move out of casting range. About ninety percent of the time I fish the Ballistic Missiles with a single hook, but they also come rigged with a treble hook, and I will have a couple in my tackle box for when fish or a hookup are hard to come by. If you are fishing from the beach and getting one bluefish is a priority, for dinner or otherwise, it may be wise to start with a treble and then switch to a single once your fish is in your cooler. When using a treble hook, you can expect your hook up rate to increase significantly.

Large metal spoons such as Hopkins and Kastmasters are also excellent choices for bluefish. They are especially productive off the beach, and they are effective when retrieved at a much slower pace than surface offerings. That can be very important if you want to put in some time casting, because cranking in Ballistic Missiles will wear you out rapidly, and if you are not getting worn out, you are not cranking fast enough. Metal spoons are also an effective choice if you suspect there are some stripers in the area and you are going for a mixed bag.

Bluefish have the reputation of eating anything, and for the most part, that reputation is largely deserved. When selecting a bluefish lure, before attempting to match the hatch or determine what the most realistic offering would be, first consider attracting the fish's attention (surface commotion), covering a lot of ground, (heavy metal lures) and whether or not you want a bluefish to eat the lure you are considering. A bluefish will usually be happy to inhale a soft plastic, but do you want to go through a new one with every strike? A bluefish will probably devour a Yo-Zuri Crystal Minnow or a Bomber, but do you want to deal with a couple treble hooks embedded near the razor sharp teeth of a fish that is not going to calmly let you unhook it?

When a bluefish is hooked on a Ballistic Missile or a metal lure with one hook in the rear, the lure itself will be what is proximate and exposed to the fish's mouth. The fish probably will not be teething the leader for the entire fight, but a leader is necessary nonetheless. During your retrieve, fish may be slashing at your plug from all angles, and a single strand main line is not going to last long. The fish's razor sharp teeth may severe you line completely without you feeling a bite. Also, bluefish are so aggressive they will often take a swipe at a lure in another's mouth. It is unlikely once you have a fish hooked that he will be able to get his teeth on the leader, but it is very likely another nearby blue will take a swipe at the lure and inadvertently liberate your hooked fish along with your lure.

I like to use about three feet of one hundred pound test mono for my leaders. I find that you get a couple more bites with mono than wire on the tough days, but the main reason I prefer it is because it is easier to handle a hooked fish on a heavy mono leader. You can take a wrap of hundred pound mono around your hand and it is not particularly unpleasant. If you take a wrap of a wire leader, at best it is going to hurt like hell, and at worst you are going to have some serious lacerations. If you do use mono rather than wire, check it frequently and retie it when necessary. The fish will knick it up, and a knicked leader will not last long.

When you get a bluefish close, be aware that the fish may get off the hook, and the pressure of the bent rod can quickly shoot the lure back toward the anglers. This is something to be aware of whenever you are fishing, but be especially careful when catching bluefish with spinning gear from a boat where the combination of the fish, the tackle and the angles involved make lures coming back into the boat a particular concern. Bluefish seem to have an endless supply of energy and usually have plenty of fight left in them when they get beside the boat. Anglers are often eager to finish the job and they exert a lot of pressure on the fish, directed toward themselves and the boat. This combined with the fact that there is not much line outside the rod and most of the stretch has been eliminated, and when the fish is right next to the boat the angles of pressure on the hook can change rapidly causing it to pull out. Under these circumstances, it is easy for the large, heavy plug with a substantial hook to come danger-ously flying back toward the angler and his companions. The entire idea of angling is to exert pressure on the fish so there is no way to eliminate it, but there are a few things you can do to minimize it. I recommend a mindset to all my clients no matter what the fishing situation. I advise you not to think of a fish fight as a test of strength, with you pulling or forcing the fish to you, but more as a test of grace and endurance where you gradu-ally convince the fish that it should come toward you. While it is going to be necessary to put pressure on a bluefish even at the end of the fight, try to lessen some of the pressure and make sure your movements are slow and even. Viciously yanking on the rod at any stage of the fight is a bad idea, and when the fish is close to the boat, it can be very dangerous. Once the fish gets close, be aware of which direction you are applying pressure, and if the hook comes out, which direction is it going to fly in. Pulling the fish right toward your face is natural, but try to change that when the fish is close. If the fish is deep, perhaps it would be possible to put some pressure on him to come up, yet slightly away from the boat. If the fish is circling, it may be possible to put sideways pressure on him and if the hook pulls, the lure will be shot harmlessly outside the boat. To boat or release the fish, a net is probably your safest option, but blues will quickly become tangled in the net, and will probably bite some bigger holes in it. I normally grab the leader, and while this puts you in harms way, if you do it right you can minimize the risk. First, wait until you have a good shot at the leader, do not spend the later half of the fight leaning over strain-ing for it. Wait until the fish is close and subdued, or as subdued as you can expect a bluefish to be, grab the leader, and immediately take a wrap or two around your hand. Unlike big-game fishing where the danger is in being pulled overboard once you get wraps, the danger here is that even with a hand on the leader, if the hook pulls the pressure from the rod is probably going to be enough to pull the leader through your hand and if that happens the chances of the hook embedding itself in your hand are excellent. As soon as you have the wraps, the angler should take all the pressure off the line, either by dropping the tip, flipping the bail, or both. Your wraps eliminate the pressure of the rod on the fish, and if the hook pulls out the lure will just dangle. You can then lift the fish into the boat or release it, just be careful of its teeth.

Getting open water bluefish to eat a fly is not particularly easy. Getting strikes in open water often depends on either creating a lot of commotion, covering a lot of ground, or both, and neither is particularly easy with a fly. Also, when you are retrieving your fly maybe fifty feet instead of a plug fifty yards, the blues tendency to follow an offering for quite some time before hitting it becomes much more of a problem and you will have many blues follow your fly to boat only to swim away when they see you. If you know you have found the fish and blind casting is not producing on the fly, try teasing them in. It is a two-person job so you will need a fishing partner. Have your partner put a Ballistic Missile or other fast-retrieved popper without a hook on a spinning rod, cast it out and reel it in at full speed. If there are bluefish around, they should be seen attacking the popper again and again, and your partner should just continue reeling. Once the popper is in range, cast your fly right behind it and start stripping, while your partner just reels the popper all the way in. One or more of the bluefish following the popper will probably veer off to eat your fly. Any patience they may have had to follow an offering is gone and they are at their most voracious having already been excited for some time by the popper. If you are having trouble with timing, it is also possible to cast your fly first, and then have your friend retrieve the popper over your fly.

When you are fly fishing for blues, use a wire shock tippet of six to ten inches. Since the fly is likely to be in their mouth, and the line right on their teeth, blues will often bite through even a heavy monofilament shock tippet. If you are casting to visible fish or fishing a rip, you may want to experiment with flies until you find something they really pounce on without hesitation, whereas if you tease them in, they will bite just about anything that is moving. Deceivers, Surf Candies, or any squid imitation is a good bet, and I would use something a little larger than the natural bait in the area to be sure the fly gets noticed. Poppers can also be a good choice, but the hook-up rate is not as good as a subsurface fly.

Summertime Bluefish

As spring passes by and the days become more uniformly sunny and warm the bluefish often move in and become more predictable. While open water continues to be a great spot to find bluefish, look for them to be stacked up in rips, especially Great Point and the Old Man by mid-July.

In my own mental fishing calendar, which is pretty fluid and flexible by necessity, open to changes based on current reports, I am currently planning on mid to late July as a time to focus much of my efforts on bluefish. Despite my eager praise of bluefish, the fact remains that my attentions will probably be devoted to flats stripers in June, Great Point stripers in early July, and the bonito bar will begin to beckon in August. While striped bass fishing will probably have slowed down, and bonito will have yet to arrive, mid summer is great time to fish for bluefish, and if you do, it will likely result in a few of the most action packed and exciting days of your summer.

Great Point

Trolling for bluefish at Great Point is the quintessential 2½ -hour Straight Wharf charter boat experience. You leave Straight Wharf for the twenty to forty minute ride (depending on the boat and the conditions), arrive at Great Point, set out hoochies on conventional rods, and troll for an hour or an hour and a half, probably take a little time to get some pictures of the lighthouse and the ever-present (and increasingly problematic) seals, and head back to the dock. You get an entire fishing experience neatly packaged into 2½ hours, and available at per-person or private boat rates. Often mockingly referred to as the "bluefish bus," both captains and anglers sometimes deride it, but it is very hard to argue with consistency or effectiveness of the trip. Nowhere else that I know of are you likely to find such a short, convenient trip with such a high rate of success. In most locales, a 2½ hour fishing charter is unheard of, a half-day being the shortest trip available. The fishing at Great Point can be good and bad, but even on bad days you are likely to tangle with a few blues. The good days are ridiculous. About six or seven years ago there a was a stretch of about four or five days when it would have been difficult to cram another bluefish into the edge of Great Point with a crowbar. If you threw a rock into the edge, it would have hit one blue and ricocheted into another before sinking. In order to keep things interesting when the fishing was almost too easy, it quickly became a contest among the captains to see how many we could release in a standard 2½ trip. As the catch tally moved past thirty and forty fish into the fifties and sixties, the key was not finding the fish or getting them to bite, that was a given. The only test was how much stamina your anglers had and how quickly you could release fish and get the lures back in the water. The top mark kept getting broken, and one day my charter was five guys in their twenties with plenty of stamina and we had a perfect west tide. My mate spent the entire trip just unhooking fish and counting them as the guys reeled non-stop. Once the hoochie was twenty feet behind the boat it usually took less than five seconds to get a bite. At the end of the 2½ hours, we had caught 102 bluefish. Given a half-hour run out and back, that means ninety minutes of fishing time and one bluefish every fifty-three seconds. That trip says a lot about trolling for bluefish at Great Point, both good in that the fishing can be good beyond all reasonable limits, and bad in that it can be a little assembly line-ish and begs the question how truly worthwhile can an experience be if can be accomplished every fifty-three seconds? To be fair however, all of the factors detracting from the experience were self-imposed, mainly the use of heavy-tackle and trolling rather than casting. In any case, we were young and it was there to be done, we did it, and I will never do it again. For a more realistic day-to-day picture, I would say that seven or eight blues in 2½ hours would be considered pretty slow fishing and twenty being pretty good fishing.

When trolling Great Point for bluefish, the key to success most of the time is keeping your lures in the right location along the edge, much the same as striper fishing in rips. However the bluefish will be a little more forgiving and little more likely to bite a lure well behind or in front of the edge. Fishing three lines is a good starting point, and having the one on the rip side the shortest, the middle line at the middle length and the outside line the longest is my preferred method *(diagram)*. The tide will pull all your lures into the rip and tangles will be kept to a minimum, at least until you get a bite.

While both tides can be excellent, generally speaking the west (outgoing) tide is more consistent for catching bluefish. It is also easier to troll the rip on the west tide because it forms a more continuous edge, whereas on the east tide, the rip forms a series of smaller edges, making it impossible to keep you lures consistently in the edge. Both the east and west tides are preferable to slack tide, but if you do find yourself there on slack tide with no rip made-up, just use the same techniques you would use to find fish in open water and a few fish can still often be found.

While three hoochies is an easy and effective way to catch some fish, mixing it up a little can be effective as well. My casting go-to, the Ballistic Missile, can draw some attention on tough days. I will run a ballistic missile either a little behind the edge, or a little in front of it because the wave action of the edge itself often caused a surface lure to tumble and tangle. Also, as I mentioned earlier in the striped bass section, swimming plugs, metal spoons, and parachute jigs will be attacked with ferocity by bluefish and they also increase your odds at getting a striper or two.

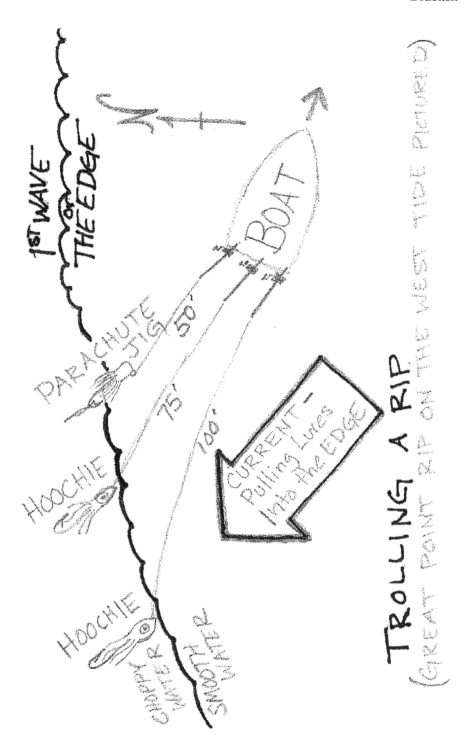

1ST WAVE or THE EDGE

N

BOAT

PARACHUTE JIG

50'

75'

100'

HOOCHIE

HOOCHIE

CHOPPY WATER

SMOOTH WATER

CURRENT — Pulling Lures Into the EDGE

TROLLING A RIP
(GREAT POINT RIP ON THE WEST TIDE PICTURED)

While trolling the edge at Great Point is great way to cover ground, locate fish and consistently catch them even though they may be spread out along the edge, casting can be effective as well. Combining a number of previously discussed methods is going to help you effectively cast for bluefish at Great Point. First, look for the fish. While seeing the fish in the edge will certainly help you if you are trolling, pinpointing the fish is more critical when casting. To spot a bluefish in the rip, you are looking for the fish itself. Fins and shadows on the bottom will probably not be visible and they should not be your focus. Concentrate most of your efforts on the first wave of the edge, which will often have more translucency that the surrounding water because of the light penetrating the wave from more angles. The fish are often visible in the first wave, usually appearing as a dark silloutte, and they appear to be surfing, just under the face of the wave.

The methods discussed in finding stripers in rips and for finding bluefish in open water will both be effective in pinpointing fish bluefish at Great Point. Bird activity is excellent. Often the birds will lead you right to the section of the rip that is productive. Idiosyncracies in the rip, such as little corners and turns concentrate fish more than a long, straight section of the edge. While slicks do not really form in the edge, they can certainly alert you to some feeding north or south of it. Do not hesitate to troll the edge upon arriving, and then cast once you have located the fish.

You run into the same issues casting for bluefish at Great Point that were discussed in casting for stripers there. If you see some fish on the edge, stop your boat and cast to them, you will have time for one or two good casts before the tide carries you through the edge, past the good fishing, and scattering the fish there. Having someone run the boat and keep it in front of the edge will make it possible to have your lures in the edge most of the time. Running out in front of the edge, and getting a few casts as you drift through it is also possible, and in fact you can often make some very long, yet productive drifts. Some days all of your bites are going to come in the little window of a few feet in front of the edge to a few feet behind it, but bluefish are much more likely than stripers to stray from the edge. Sometimes you can go a hundred yards or more off the edge and have consistent fishing drifting all the way back to it, and perhaps even on the back side of it.

When casting for blues at Great Point (or any fish at any rip), keep in mind that they will be facing into the tide, looking out in front of the rip, and that all the bait and prey is going to be approaching them from this direction. While I advocated casting well beyond bluefish in open water and retrieving your lure across their path, do not throw your lure back across the rip and pull it out. It will be approaching the fish from behind a direction that no natural bait would come from, they will not be looking for it in order to eat it, and they may be scared off by it. Cast out in front of the rip edge and let the tide carry your lure back into and across the edge. Your lure is going to be getting swept toward the edge in the same manner of the natural bait in the area, and the bluefish are going to be looking for it in the right place.

Casting at Great Point would probably be the only place where a Ballistic Missile would not be my first choice. Using a lure that is effective when retrieved at slower speeds will give you a little more versatility when fishing the edge. You can slow your retrieve to let the tide pull your lure into the strike zone or to let your lure linger in a productive spot, and you can quicken your retrieve to get in front of fish, all the while having it remain an enticing offering, whereas a Ballistic Missile becomes less appealing every time you slow it down. The distinct possibility of a few stripers being present is also a consideration, and in late summer and the fall, bonito and false albacore become a possibility as well. A Hopkins or Deadly Dick is a good choice. A swimming plug is also a good choice, though I would recommend removing some of the hooks or replacing the trebles with singles. Topwater is still a great option and needlefish or chugger-style floating poppers are excellent choices.

Great Point from the Shore

Surf casting from Great Point is a classic island fishing activity, and can be fantastic. The most popular spot is along the northwest side, abutting deep water. The Galls, both the ocean side and Chord of the Bay side, are good options as well. Use the same methods mentioned earlier to locate the fish. Tackle is also the same, throw a Ballistic Missile to get their attention, or cover some ground and use a large spoon retrieved at a more leisurely pace. If nothing is showing on the surface, I would recommend the Chord of the Bay side right where the skinny Galls start to widen out. It is know as the "south parking lot" and it is a favorite of false albacore fisherman in the fall, but it is also a good, and often overlooked, spot to find a few blues in the summer. Starting there and working north toward the point is a good way to find a few fish when nothing exciting is visible.

These days, it is impossible to talk about fishing from the beach at Great Point without talking about the seals. The population of seals has skyrocketed in the last ten years, and many of them now make their home on the tip of Great Point for the entire summer. There is also a huge colony of them on Muskeget, there are often a few at Bigelow's Point on Tuckernuck, they can be found at Smith's Point, and sighting them anywhere along Nantucket's shores has become commonplace. There are many valid concerns about the effect of their overpopulation especially as regards to the vast amounts of smaller fish they consume and the taxing effects of this on the ecosystem. The percentage of seals' diet made up of striped bass and bluefish is a matter of debate. Scientific analysis of seal scat reveals it contains virtually no striped bass bones, but fisherman point out that seals tend to eat the fish's boneless belly and discard the head and bones. Anybody who had spent time on the water in recent years has seen striper carcasses, gnawed to the head and spine by a seal, and discarded. While I think most people agree that striped bass and bluefish are not the bulk of a seal's diet, there is no doubt that a seal will happily and quickly grab a hooked fish if given the chance. I have had seals grab hooked fish at Great Point and in the Chord of the Bay, but in a boat it is only an occasional occurrence. If you are surf casting, getting a fish past the seals to the beach at Great Point is always a concern, and at times over the past couple years, it has been impossible. Usually, the seals make there home right at the tip of the point, and the area has been roped off to keep the seals interaction with people at a minimum. The rope and the seals make fishing the first part of the rip's edge an impossibility. Moving south down the east or west sides of the Point will get you away from the bulk of the seals, though more often than not, there will be a few cruising the shore.

While I wouldn't fish amongst a large number of seals, I also would not let sighting of few seals prevent me from fishing where I otherwise wanted to. In years before populations reached the current problematic levels, some beach anglers would claim seals were a good sign. I would agree to the point that generally when fishing, any life is good life and to find an area where the food chain is hopping is good. On the other hand, if too many seals are around, the fish are probably more concerned with avoiding becoming a meal than finding their next one, as is probably the case off the tip of Great Point most of the time.

If you do hook a fish in the vicinity of seals the only thing you can do is try to make the fight as quick as possible. Set your drag as tightly as you can and really put some pressure on the fish. The longer your fish struggles in the water, the more attention it is going to attract. In the tropics, if you are fishing on the flats and a shark is visible and in hot pursuit of your hooked fish, free-spooling your rod will give your fish a chance to outrun the shark. I have not heard of this method being employed to thwart seal attacks, but if you see a seal coming for your fish, it may be worth a shot as a last resort. If a seal does grab your fish, I would recommend pointing your rod at the seal and grabbing your spool to force the issue right away: either your line will break, the hook will pull, or rarely, the fish will be pulled away from the seal. Regardless of the outcome, nothing good can come of you staying attached to the seal. While it is hard to argue with a seal's cuteness, they are large, powerful, aggressive, and they have quite a set of jaws.

In the last couple years there has been some discussion of thinning the seal population. There are tremendous difficulties with this being because, despite their overpopulation, seals are afforded a great deal of federal protection. Mother Nature is trying to rectify the problem and great whites have become a staple off Chatham (just a few miles north of Great Point). It is going to take a lot of great whites quite some time to put a dent in the amount of seals, but they are doing their best.

The Old Man

When I am fishing new water, I often find myself looking for easy, consistent action. There are no guarantees in fishing, but I am looking for the next best thing, some high probability fishing, easy to figure out, and not necessarily for the top-billed sportfish of the area. When I was first fishing Southwest Florida, snook fishing may have been excellent, but even then it took precision and local knowledge to find them consistently, and if hungry jacks, ladyfish and the occasional sea trout were feeding under easily found birds, I was just as happy to bend my rod there. When I think of the Nantucket solution to this fishing circumstance, a desire for some consistent action without the need for a tremendous amount of precision and an extremely high likelihood of fish being present, I think of bluefish on the Old Man Shoal in the summer.

The big rip is the first to fill with stripers in spring and gradually, usually over the course of a few weeks more and more bluefish arrive and stay the summer. However, there are significant drawbacks, which I will touch on first. The Old Man is a few miles off the Southeastern corner of Nantucket, making it a significant ride regardless of whether you leave from Madaket or town. In a twenty-knot boat it is a solid hour from town, and you can probably shave a little off that from Madaket, but not much. Running an hour to get to bluefish may not be how you want to spend your time or money, especially in these days of astronomical fuel prices. If you leave from town, you pass over potentially good bluefishing in the Chord of the Bay, Great Point, Wauwinet, and Sankaty before getting to the Old Man. If you leave from Madaket, the waters along the South Shore can also be loaded with bluefish, making a run to the Old Man superfluous. The conditions are also cause for concern, as the Old Man can be a very rough area. As I mentioned in fishing the rips for striped bass, the conditions at the rips can be dangerous even when it is placid on Nantucket, and the Old Man is among the roughest of all the rips and has some of the strongest currents. I am not going to get into specifics on what boats are too small on what days in how much wind, but I would never recommend going in a boat under twenty feet, and in anything under thirty feet I would carefully pick my days, especially until you have some experience with the area.

Now that I have addressed the drawbacks, I can move to the virtues, which are substantial. I touched upon sometimes being able to see bluefish surfing in the first wave of the rip at Great Point, and in the summer at the Old Man that is the rule rather than the exception. Almost every day you will be able to see fish surfing the edge. Some days it will be a few fish here and there, but more often than not it will be ten or twenty packed into every corner of the rip. More so than any other rip, birds, both seagulls and terns, are likely to be present and guide you right to the epicenter of the feeding. Bait is often visible getting swept across the edge, and often packs of blues race out to intercept it, boiling and busting in the calm water in front of the rip.

The bluefish at the Old Man are usually very big. Anywhere in Nantucket Sound, and at Great Point specifically you can find bluefish in all sizes. On any given day at Great Point there may be predominantly two pounders or predominately eight pounders, or at times a mixture of sizes, but the average Great Point blue is probably four or five pounds. Once you get down to Sankaty and the Old Man, the two pounders seem to disappear and most of the fish you encounter are going to be a solid eight pounds, with plenty of ten-plus pounders mixed in.

You may encounter a boat or two trolling the Old Man with wire line. That is the best bet if you are hoping to pull out a striper, of which there is a possibility all summer. Wire will be an effective way to catch bluefish too, and those sticking with wire in hopes of the striper in the summer are likely to catch at least twenty bluefish for every striper, and that one striper is by no means a guarantee. By no means is wire necessary though, the bluefish are feeding throughout the water column and light tackle on the surface is very effective. It is very likely that your choice of offering is not going to matter at all; competition amongst the myriad of bluefish for a meal brings their voracity to a whole new level. Instead, choose your lure based on durability, your ability to keep it in the strike zone, and one single hook. Spoons, poppers, Ballistic Missiles, and swimming plugs and needlefish rerigged with a single hook are all excellent choices.

Fish it in the same manner as Great Point and the other rips, either trolling or casting or both. When you hook a fish, especially on light tackle, it is probably going to be necessary to get back behind the edge, as pulling the fish through the edge will be impossible. Use caution getting through the edge, and do not hesitate to drive the boat around and go through the edge bow-first. You do not want to take a breaker over the transom, which is certainly a possibility at the Old Man.

All the other outer rips will hold bluefish from time to time, though I would not recommend a trip there to target them. More consistent action is generally available closer to home.

The Airport and the South Shore

When I was in high school, I mated for a retired gentleman who kept his boat in Madaket, and about three or four times a week all summer long we went down off the airport fished for bluefish. It was two great summers of fishing, and almost every day we found them tailing. He would just drive east along the south shore and my young eyes would find the tails, and when we found them, my boss and his guests would throw Ballistic Missiles at them. Sometimes the fishing would slow down and we would take a little ride to find more tailers, but usually we would just drift amongst fish all day, never needing to start the motor again until it was time to head home.

It has been a long time since I have fished the airport for bluefish always departing from town when the target was bluefish and never giving any thought to venturing past the Old Man, but I know it can still be very good from time to time, and some summers offer the consistency I found there for a couple years. Fishing most of the South Shore is about finding the fish in open water, but Miacomet Rip can hold fish, and that can be fished in the same manner as the Old Man.

Fall Bluefishing

Bluefishing in the fall is more of the same. Fish will continue to feed in the rips and they will continue to be found in open water. Great Point will usually remain fairly consistent, with a few fish to be had most days and some really excellent days as well. The Old Man will still hold some bluefish, though their numbers will drop off significantly as they will share the rip with stripers again.

Beach fishing is likely to heat up in the fall as schools of fish become more active in their pursuit of bait as they head south. Nantucket Harbor often fills up with tinker-blues, little guys just a few ounces and maybe six or eight inches, and schools of bluefish of two or three pounds are often found all over the channels around Madaket Harbor, Tuckernuck and Eel Point. The tinker blues in town are fun for kids, and they usually happily eat pieces of squid fished from a dock, and the little guys in Madaket perform admirably on ultra light gear.

CHAPTER THREE

Bonito

I love bonito. I would not be able to say that I look forward to their arrival with as much anticipation as the stripers, because by the time bonito come into the picture, I have three solid months of fishing behind me, whereas the prelude to stripers is six months of cold and fishlessness interrupted only by trips south. I would not even be comfortable choosing bonito over stripers if forced to choose only one to pursue, given that striped bass are present for six months and if bonito last longer than a month that is a good showing. Any definitive, superlative statement regarding the bonito is difficult, but what I will say is that when they arrive, I am far more likely to be on the Bonito Bar for the day's incoming tide than anywhere else, regardless of whether I have clients or not. Once hooked their fight is as exciting as any fish you care to name. They make lightning fast runs and their power is reminiscent of their larger cousins in the tuna family. They also change directions faster and more abruptly than any fish I have ever caught. They are perfectly suited to light spinning gear and fly rods. The height of bonito fishing also coincides nicely with the height of Nantucket's tourist season, mid-August, and the best spot to find them is the easily accessible and aptly named Bonito Bar, just outside Smith's Point.

At least when compared to many mainland fishing locales, fishing in a crowd and fighting other anglers to get into spots is, luckily, not something we need to worry a great deal about. Great Point Rip on good weather weekends can get a little crowded and if a good striper bite draws commercial fishermen to Sankaty or the eastern shore fishing there will quickly get pretty tight and ruthless, but the tightest bumper-to-bumper fishing you will find around the island is undoubtedly the Bonito Bar, August weekends, with an incoming tide.

It probably will not be so bad that you can't get a spot a to fish, but it is a distinct possibility you will need to aim your casts so as not to hit the surrounding boats. Probably the key reason for the Bonito Bar's popularity is that it is virtually the only place around Nantucket to find them with any kind of regularity. That is not to say they are not found elsewhere or caught from the beach, they most certainly are. Nantucket Harbor has not had a consistent bonito bite in a few years, but when I was a kid big schools of them used to bust bait in the jetties and in the anchorage, especially in the early morning and most of the island's bonito fishing took place there rather than the Bonito Bar. Some bonito are always caught at Great Point, both from boats fishing the edge and from surf fisherman along both sides of the point and down to the south parking lot. That being said, if you are targeting bonito, any plan other than to be at the Bonito Bar for the incoming tide is something of a long shot. Whereas I could name fifty different spots around Nantucket that would be reasonable places to expect to catch striped bass, for bonito there is only one.

The Bonito Bar is large and loosely defined area south of Madaket Beach, east of the sandbars that border the cut between Smith's Point and Tuckernuck. Use caution going to through the cut, drastic depth changes, strong currents and large breakers are the norm. Once you get through the cut, get safely east of the breakers, and you are on the Bonito Bar. Especially when you are new to an area, other boats fishing can be a wonderful indicator of fish, and even on a weekday you will probably not be alone on the Bonito Bar. Use common sense and good manners to determine how close is too close given the conditions and the amount of boats in the area. The sandbars around the cut are on average about three to five feet deep, and that is where the large swells will be breaking. The water then drops off again to roughly six to ten feet, and while you can travel over these areas, you do not want to linger in them and certainly never anchor in them because of the swells. As you continue south or east depths slide to an average of about fifteen feet and fairly quickly to twenty-five, and the area around this drop off is usually where you are going to find the fish.

When you arrive at the Bonito Bar, spend some time looking into the water and you will hopefully see what makes it the bonito capital of Nantucket, and perhaps the world. Usually, huge schools of sand eels are all over the place. They are so tightly packed they darken the water, and you will see the dark circles milling around. They come to the surface and make a bubbling sound, as if the entire Bonito Bar were a freshly poured Sprite. They are so thick it is not uncommon to inadvertently impale a few while retrieving your fly or lure. Once they get higher than a few thousand, numbers get fairly abstract to me, but if I had to guess I would say that the number of sand eels at the Bonito Bar on a typical August incoming tide is in the millions. That may be totally wrong, but even if it is, there are still enough sand eels there to make me believe there are millions.

The most popular method of fishing the bar is to anchor and cast. Upon arriving, I usually observe the birds for a while. Besides getting attacked from below by the fish the sand eels are in peril from the hundreds of birds usually present. Seagulls and shearwaters are there at times, and terns are there consistently. I try to determine if there is a specific section of the bar where the birds and bait are heaviest. Do not be concerned with your exact placement, and precision in regards to both your boat and your casts is not necessary. The Bonito Bar itself has very vague and fluid boundaries, it is much more of a general area that one specific spot. The bait, the birds and

119

the fish will be all mixed up racing around the area, usually in a seemingly random manner. Just pick a lively area and put your time in.

When I began targeting bonito fairly often about eight or nine years ago, it was widely held that trolling was ineffective, and bonito were so skittish that a running engine would send them scurrying before they ever got a look at your lures. Anybody trolling the Bonito Bar was sure to get some hairy eyeballs from the anchored casters. Over the last few seasons, that has changed. Trolling for bonito has proven very effective, and given its effectiveness trolling the Bonito Bar has become both common and acceptable. I still prefer to cast for them and especially to fly fish for them, but much like when finding bluefish in open water, trolling a few lines can help you locate the fish. When I arrive at the bar and ride around surveying the bait and the birds, I usually toss a couple lines out as well, stopping to cast if we get a hook up. There are also some days, for reasons that I have trouble putting my finger on, trolling just out-produces casting. I will arrive, get a bite trolling, stop and cast with no results, and return to trolling and immediately get bites again.

While trolling the Bonito Bar is certainly not the taboo it once was, motoring around a bunch of anchored or drifting anglers requires some tact and common sense. Give all the non-trolling boats wide berth. If there are more than a few boats situated along the bar, I will generally troll in deeper water east or south of all of them, and perhaps move into shallower water if there are no other boats for a significant stretch. Trolling in and around other boats is definitely something that should be avoided.

The vast majority of the fishing at the Bonito Bar is blind. In many locations, bonito fishing is all about surface blitzes and getting your offering into one whether that be by correctly anticipating where one will take place or, failing that, running and gunning. While fish at the Bonito Bar will occasionally come to the surface in an all out blitz, most of the time they will not show themselves and when they do it will be the occasional swirl or solitary splash. Certainly, if a fish swirls or splashes within range, cast to the area and if a blitz happens within range try to land your lure in the maylay, but do not count on seeing fish. Just put in your time blind casting among the birds and the bait; the bites will come.

I first started encountering bonito in Nantucket Harbor in the late summer, in the 1990s when their presence there was much more consistent. I saw a lot of them and caught none of them, leading me to read about them. I recall the recommendations of the day being to match the hatch, and try to imitate sand eels with tiny silver offerings. Swedish Pimples and tiny Hopkins where the lures of choice and small Epoxy Minnows were the favored fly, and silver flash was thought to be good. These days on the Bonito Bar, the fish and I both still love the silver flash, but I would not recommend you go to tremendous lengths in an attempt to match the hatch. As I said earlier, on an average day in August, the number of sand eels in the water is astounding. I believe that the better your bait blends in with the natural baits, the better chance it has of being just another sand eel in the crowd. It does not matter how many hungry bonito are feeding on the bar, if your lure is just another sand eel in the crowd, the odds are not in your favor. I would recommend something that sticks out a little bit. I think of it as choosing something that a bonito will notice amongst clouds of natural bait, and while it is different, it is similar in some way critical way that triggers the bonito to attack it once it is noticed. Now, without getting into the fish's mind, I cannot say if that is actually what goes on, but I can say that it has been very successful.

My first choice for a lure on the Bonito Bar is a 5¼-inch Yo-Zuri Crystal Minnow in any of the colors that have silver sides, such as the mackerel, black back and silver and red head. I prefer the sinking ones, but floating ones work well too. It is significantly bigger than a sand-eel and it throws off a tremendous amount of flash to ensure that is noticed. It does have a fairly slim profile, reminiscent of a sand-eel, and in my experience the fish prefer this lure to any other.

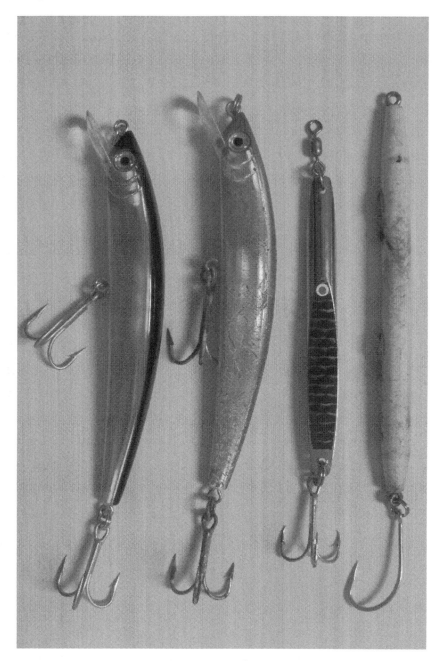

Bonito and False Albacore Lures

Left to Right: Yo-Zuri Crystal Minnow (black back, sinking), Used Crystal Minnow complete with bonito scars (blue/purple back, sinking), Deadly Dick, Spofford's Needlefish

Another favorite lure of mine is a needlefish, and in particular the Spofford's Needlefish. It is retrieved quickly on the surface in a fashion similar to the Ballistic Missile, yet your retrieve can be a little slower and the surface action is more subtle. Bonito will only rarely take a loud surface popper, but a needlefish sliding gently along the surface gets their attention and induces strikes. One drawback to the Spofford's Needlefish is that it comes rigged with three little treble hooks. I find the hooks to be too numerous and not stout enough. I have found that a single hook on the back is nearly as effective at hooking fish, and far more effective at landing them once they are hooked. A Hogy can also provide a subtle surface disturbance that effectively attracts bonito.

The Deadly Dick is another excellent bonito lure. Its skinny profile is very similar to a sand eel and it throws a lot of flash.

If you are throwing a fly, a white bonito bunny has always been my favorite. When I tie them, I like to add a little blue, green and silver flash. My aforementioned chunky sand eel pattern also comes out of the box quite often with good results. Skok's Mushmouths throw out a tremendous amount of flash, and have been a very popular choice as of late. Even if you are spinfishing, consider adding one of the above flies as a teaser above your lure.

Bonito have excellent vision and they are certainly leader shy. I use about three feet of 25lbs. fluorocarbon, which is light enough. They have very sharp teeth, but they are more needle-like than a blue's and getting bit off by a bonito should not be a huge concern. Often times though, there are bluefish on the bonito bar as well, and then you do have to worry about getting bit off. While getting a Hogy sliced is inconvenient, having Crystal Minnows bitten off with any regularity can put your child's college tuition in jeopardy. Fishing single hooks, or at least removing the front treble hook, in order to keep the lure in between the fish and the fluorocarbon can help, but it may be necessary to beef up your leader. Going to up to fifty or sixty pounds will probably eliminate the cut-offs as long as you check

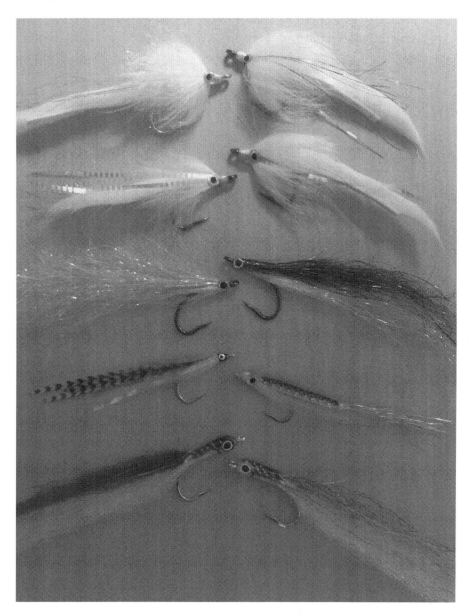

My Favorite Bonito and False Albacore Flies

Top to Bottom: Bonito Bunny with a incorporated blue flash, Bonito Bunny with incorporated green flash, Bonito Bunny with prismatic sides, Bonito Bunny with lateral scale flash sides, Skok's Mushmouth with a purple back, Skok's Mushmouth with a green back, Deceiver Variation with fish hair and chartreuse and black barred feathers, Boyle's Albie Fly, Chunky Sand Eel with a blue back, Chunky Sand Eel with a green back it frequently for nicks and scrapes, and you can still expect some bonito bites. I would not recommend going to wire. I also now consistently net the bluefish when they are brought to the boat. I have come to this necessary inconvenience after grabbing the leader and lifting only to watch several bluefish unceremoniously plop back into the water with my lure still in their maw. Bluefish do not lend themselves to being picked up by hand out of the water, their tales are too streamlined and flimsy to get a grip on, and your certainly do not want your hand anywhere near their jaws. Often during the fight the blue will have nicked or scratched the already light leader, and trying to pluck the fish out of the water with the leader is too much for it. Netting bluefish is a tremendous hassle, and they often immediately tangle themselves and the lure up in the net, sometimes chomping holes in it, but it saves a lot of tackle and the fish can be released unencumbered.

When casting, vary your retrieve until you find what works. If you are certain fish are around and feeding, start with a fast retrieve. Bonito are real speedsters; they are going to be able to catch your offering if they want to regardless of how fast you reel, and having your lure race through the water really turns them on. If nothing is putting you on high alert, a nice steady retrieve will certainly produce results. While I have never had consistent success with a slow retrieve, fish will definitely hit something that is not being retrieved at all, especially a Yo-Zuri or a fly. On occasion, a client or I will stop our retrieve for one reason or another, and after a few seconds of motionlessness, a bonito will absolutely hammer it. When trolling, sometimes you are forced to make a hard turn and you will get bites on the turn as your lures lie motionless. My theory is that among the myriad of sand eels the bonito pick out these slowly sinking offerings as easy targets. I would not advise throwing out a lure and letting it sit indefinitely, but do not hesitate to add some five to ten second pauses to your retrieves from time to time.

Once you hook a bonito, the fun really begins. Be prepared for a long run, but be equally prepared for that run to stop immediately and for you to be left with slack line. For those not familiar with bonito, their first thought upon feeling the sudden slack line is that the fish is off. That is usually not the case, and the bonito has just changed directions abruptly. Start taking in the slack as fast as possible, and get ready for the line to come tight on the fish. It can be particularly exciting to watch your line come back to the boat and then come tight as the fish scoots right by in the opposite direction. Be prepared to move around your boat. Always try to keep as little of the boat as possible in between you and the fish, that is to say, if you hook the fish in the bow and it races to the stern, make your way to the stern as well. You do not want your line running over the boat to avoid tangles and for safety sake, and if the fish turns back toward the bow, it is likely your line is going to find its way around some underwater portion of your boat, and the fish will break you off. This is true for all species and you always want to eliminate as much of the boat between you and the fish as possible, but no other species will test you on it like bonito. Often, these quick directional changes take a course under your boat, and if that happens, do not hesitate to stick your entire rod in the water almost up to the reel. Rods are waterproof. If you do not put your rod into the water, it will be bending at an extreme and unnatural angle that could cause it break, your line will rub on the bottom of your boat, and that could cause it to part, and pressure could be lost on the fish, making it easy for the fish to throw the hook. If you put your rod in the water, an uninterrupted line from the rod to the fish will still exist, and you can still exert pressure on the fish. You can try to work yourself around to the other side of the boat, which can be difficult especially if engines are not tilted up or an anchor line is involved, or you can play the fish with your rod in the water until it returns to your side.

FIGHTING A FISH THAT HAS SWAM UNDER THE BOAT

WRONG

RIGHT

Extreme rod bend

FRICTION & ABRASION

Straight and tight line to Fish

127

As summer turns to fall, bonito fishing gets a little more unpredictable. It is a possibility that the fish will vanish at the first hint of cold or bad weather and not be seen again until next August, but more often a few stick around into the fall, and bonito fishing has been good well into September in recent years. When August turns to September, you will probably encounter better days at Great Point both near the Point itself and in the south parking lot. In Madaket, the incoming tide on the bar ceases to be the only game in town and you may be able to find them more frequently on different tides and in and around the channel between Smith's Point and Tuckernuck and the channel around Eel Point. Bonito also pop up from time to time offshore in the Rose & Crown and the 6 Can. While there has not been a particularly good harbor bonito bite the past few years a few fish have been found in the harbor in the fall. The Bonito Bar remains a good option, though it too becomes more unpredictable in the fall. While it is going to produce most days in August, once the fall arrives, it is going to be much more hit or miss. In seasons past, I have prematurely quit on the Bonito Bar more than once, having fished it with no luck for a few days in September and decided there were no more fish there, only to have it light back up again a day or a week later when I am elsewhere.

CHAPTER FOUR

False Albacore

W hile I have been contemplating this book for a number of years, and doing some scribbling for nearly all of them, I am writing this in early 2012. If I had been a little less busy, or perhaps more focused, a computer not had an ill-timed crash, and for whatever other reasons, if I had accomplished this writing in 2011, the false albacore section would have been quite a bit different. The best albie fishing I have ever witnessed, and probably the best the island has ever seen, took place in the fall of 2011. I spent a lot of early September stuck at the dock and a little writing got done, and in looking over what I wrote, I think it gives you a compelling picture of the nature of albie fishing. Here it is:

Some years in late August or early September, both bonito and false alba-core are feeding on the sand eels present at the Bonito Bar, and when that happens, fishing can be incredible. In 2009 the Bonito Bar was as good I have ever seen it in my lifetime for about three days in early September, with bonito and false albacore mixed together. As I write this, it is early September 2011, the wind has blowing out of the Northeast for three days, murky water is still lingering around the island from Hurricane Irene, and as far as I know, nobody has caught a false albacore yet.

The tone is pessimistic to say the least. Being stuck in your house can do that to you, but at that point there was no reason to be optimistic and it looked as though a false albacore run of any size may pass the island by. However, shortly after that writing, the weather got better and the water cleared up. Bonito surprised a lot of people by reappearing, bad weather in late summer often being the impetus for their departure. Albies started showing here and there, and then it turned into a wide-open bite on both ends of the island that lasted for weeks. In Nantucket's 2011 *Inshore Classic*, a month long tournament that concluded October 15th, seventy-two false albacore were weighed-in, the most in tournament history, compared to sixty-one bluefish, seventeen bonito and only twenty-one stripers.

False albacore are about as unpredictable as fish get. Compared to false albacore, you could set your watch by fickle and finicky bonito. For every other inshore fish on Nantucket, I can give you a place, a time of year, and maybe a tide, and feel very comfortable and confident that there are going to be a least a few fish there. That is most certainly not the case for albies, and while I will still offer you some locations, time and tides, there is the distinct possibility of arriving to a seemingly life-less bit of ocean and having no bites at all. The bottom line is that if you are going to fish for false albacore, you need to be ready to take some skunkings. A lot of waiting and watching for albies, whether you do it walking, floating, casting or trolling, can make you question whether albies are the best use of your time, and whether there is something more productive you could be doing on or off the water. But when they do show up, they are quick to show or remind you that they are a fish worth waiting for.

The charter business on Nantucket slows down quite a bit at the end of August when kids go back to school, and beach and sun loving vacationers look southward. There are still plenty of fish and fisherman, but the hectic pace of August gives way to some free time in September and mostly free time by October. In 2011, luckily for him, Mike Schuster, had completed his higher education. In the fine tradition of fishing-bums, he was not pursuing a career, but staying on Nantucket to get acquainted with the fall fishing that he missed all of those years leaving for college in late August. In mid-September we spent a few days bobbing around Great Point, in the usual false albacore haunts, casting, trolling, and looking with a few bluefish to show for our efforts. We had caught a few albacore together before with clients, and they were impressive enough, but Mike wondered if all this bobbing around was worth it, and was considering a return to New Hampshire. Then I got a good report about false albacore as well as a lingering bonito bite on the west end. The next day we headed to Madaket and Mike got into a couple on the fly, and was immediately as hooked as the fish. When he had a moment to think about it, he quickly acknowledged that all the bobbing, waiting and looking was worth it. He also said that he could see why the fish was captivating saltwater fly fisherman nationwide, he put off leaving the island as long as possible, and starting considering a trip to Harker's Island, North Carolina, the epicenter of albie fishing.

False albacore are similar to bonito in size and appearance, but easy to tell apart if you know what to look for. Bonito have stripes running almost laterally on their backs and they are barred vertically with dark triangles. On some fish, the stripes are prominent and on others the dark barring is more prominent. False albacore have a patch on their back that is filled with little dark squiggles. Bonito have sharp, needle-like teeth, and false albacore have only dull little nubs, and are often described as toothless. False albacore also tend to be slightly larger and more football shaped, whereas bonito tend to stay fairly slim.

Bonito and False Albacore, Which is Which?

Their fighting style is very similar. False albacore will make longer runs, and of all the inshore species, they are the most likely to spool you. They also have more stamina than a bonito. While they will make quick direction changes, they do not do it as often or as abruptly as bonito, and I would give a very slight nod to bonito in terms of sheer speed.

Their biggest difference is in their desirability as table fare, and hence where being able to tell them apart is the most important. Bonito meat is similar in taste and texture to other small members of the tuna family. The meat is white or pale pink rather than the red meat of its larger cousins yellowfin and bluefin, and it tastes a lot like yellowfin tastes when it is cooked all the way through rather than the more popular rare preparations of today. False albacore walk the line between very bad and totally inedible. The entirety of their flesh is very dark meat, almost purple, and they are very oily. Aside from the very occasional fish weighed in a tournament and then recycled as bait, pet food, or fertilizer, false albacore should be released.

False albacore arrive on Nantucket usually in late August or September and usually linger until October. Often times, the first arrivals make their presence known on the Bonito Bar. In late August and early September you can sometimes encounter a nice mixed bag of both bonito and false albacore on the Bar, and since lures, flies and methods for bonito and false albacore are largely the same, there is no need to alter your methods if you know or suspect albacore are present. While it is unpredictable, the fishing has the potential to be absolutely spectacular. A few seasons ago, for three days at the end of August and beginning of September, the action was incredible. Almost every cast produced a fish, the mix probably about seventy percent bonito and thirty percent albacore. After three days the fishing dropped off as quickly as it started.

Probably the most consistent false albacore spot in recent years has been the south parking lot of Great Point. It is at the north end of the Galls on the Nantucket Sound side, rather than the Atlantic side, where the point starts to widen out. The beach faces southwest and west and it drops off fairly quickly. If you are standing on the beach throwing a Deadly Dick (the predominant offering of choice for falsies), it is probably landing in thirty feet of water. Bait tends to congregate in the area, especially in the fall, and sometimes the albies are there too. Even if albie fishing is pretty slow, putting in your time at this spot can result in picking up a few fish. In my experience, tide affects the spot very little, and while the fish may certainly pop up there at any time, early in the morning seems to produce better than the rest of the day.

Great Point itself is another spot that holds albies from time to time. Unlike bluefish and striped bass, which tend to stay in very predictable places along the rip when the tide is flowing, false albacore are liable to pop up anywhere, north of the edge, south of the edge, or right along it. Oftentimes, during the east tide at Great Point, a secondary edge makes up starting at the point and going almost straight north, as opposed to the much larger, more prominent rip that heads northeast and then east. If you are fishing the point for blues and stripers, this secondary edge is barely worth a second look, but false albacore love the secondary edge. My best day of false albacore fishing was at Great Point in 2008 during the *Redbone@Large Nantucket Slam*. If we had not been in a tournament, we probably would have stayed at the dock. The wind was blowing hard from the northeast, it was raining off and on, and the albacore continually busted bait back and forth along the secondary edge. Peter Bishop, an experienced false albacore guy, was one of the tournament anglers onboard and he showed off a great trick for busting albies. He would cast his Deadly Dick and then stick the first two eyes of his rod into the water and retrieve as fast as he was capable. Even though a Deadly Dick is a heavy, fast sinking lure, reeling it in as fast as possible will still cause it to come to the surface, splash around, and lose some of its appeal. While in many circumstances you want your lure splashing around, a Deadly Dick is most effective when under the surface. By keeping the rod tip underwater, he was able to reel as fast as possible while still keeping the lure under the surface. The fish absolutely loved the blazing retrieve and the lures subsurface action. Any angler experienced with false albacore will tell you that getting a lure into busting fish is by no means a guarantee of hook-up, but more often than not one of Peter's casts would result in a bite. He got sixteen false albacore that day and we won the tournament. In true albie fashion, subsequent trips to the same spot over the next few days offered nary a glimpse of a fish.

Heading further east, the outer rips are also good places to find false albacore, as well as the occasional big bonito, in the late summer and fall. I have always found it a little bizarre that the warm-water loving little tunas make their way out to these usually chilly waters, but they certainly do. The end of August and early September are usually when the water over these shoals is warmest, and the fish are tolerant of cooler water as long as there is food to be had, which is often the case in the outer rips, and everything tends to get a little mixed up in the fall anyway, with fish popping up in unexpected places. The most consistent of the outer rips for false albacore is the 6-Can, but they will make occasional appearances at all of them. If they are there they will usually take a Pearl Bomber and sometimes a parachute jig, but switching to a lure with more silver flash is a better way to target them.

The hottest and most consistent fishing of 2011 took place in the channel between Smith's Point and Tuckernuck. As the tide started flowing out, bait was flowing with it and pods of false albacore would bust it up. I managed to fish it five or six times in late September and early October, and with uncharacteristic predictability, the albacore were there every time. As is most often the case, the fish were moving around and going up and down very fast. However, there were a lot of fish and nearly all the activity seemed to be confined to the cut starting roughly on an imaginary line drawn from Smith's Point to the entrance of Tuckernuck Harbor, and ending up against the breakers and shallow water about a half mile south. I would stop at the imaginary line and drift south with the tide, and before reaching the breakers, run back up the side of the cut and do it again.

It was tempting, as it always is, to run within range of breaking fish and get a cast into them before they went down, but it was not effective. As is usually the case, the feeding bursts were short and running around only made them shorter. Just drifting out with the tide, favoring the side of the cut where the fish seemed most active, produced quality shots almost every drift.

The run and gun versus sit tight debate is nowhere more present than when chasing albacore, and I do not see it as a black and white issue. I think that running and gunning is the most effective option at times, and if it is done as little as possible with a bit of common sense and courtesy, the drawbacks can be largely eliminated. Sometimes, albacore are busting bait in open water without a pattern and you are going to get more shots by moving to them rather than waiting for them to come to you. Do not go right to the fish, get only to within a cast length, and if possible let the wind and tide do the final bit of the work. However, if the fish are consistently showing in the same area or in a pattern, if anchoring or drifting is an option, I would highly recommend it. The shots you get at busting fish when they come to you rather then when you go to them are going to be far superior. When you run to busting fish, you usually miss out on the best part of the bite, and running to them faster and louder only hastens their departure. When you wait and the bite materializes around you, you can take advantage of the whole thing. Also, when you are anchored or drifting, the bait may use your boat as shelter and the blitz will literally be taking place all around your boat. In early October of 2011, I was leaving town headed for the Madaket cut again, but I quickly cut my trip short because albies were busting off Brant Point. At first they were moving around randomly from the no-wake buoys in the channel all the way to south and east of First Point. They were not a ton of fish around, but there were enough to make me stay. Unable to establish a pattern, I ran to busting fish when I saw them, and I got one or two mediocre shots, and no takers. After a little while, the fish started showing with some regularity just north of the anchorage. I stopped running and just made repeated drifts thought the area. After a few uneventful drifts, I considered running to the fish again, but patience prevailed and on my next drift the blitz occurred right around my boat. I cast my bonito bunny, stripped it in fast, and then let it sit next to boat for an instant before casting again. It was hammered by a big albie. After a spirited fight, a few trips deep into the backing, and not a small amount of concern on my part that the fish would find his way around a mooring, I got it into the boat. It weighed eleven and half pounds, and took the fly rod division of the *Inshore Classic*.

A long run is certainly not necessary, and at times Nantucket Harbor is going to have the best albie fishing around. The entire area between the jetties into Brant Point, the entire anchorage and up harbor all the way to Second Point is a good place to find fish busting. Blind casting around the end of both the east and west jetty can be productive. In years past, sometimes on the falling tide albies would cruise back and forth along the east side of the East Jetty busting bait along it with some regularity. To my knowledge this has not been the case the past couple seasons, but it is worth a look.

The last place I will specifically mention as an albacore hangout is the north shore off Dionis. I have found busting albacore from the submerged rock off fortieth pole west to the Madaket Harbor entrance buoy. Usually the action is along the outer sandbar, where the depth goes from fifteen or twenty feet up to six to ten feet. In 2011 I stopped on fish busting there a couple times on my way to the Madaket cut and managed to get a fish there one day, and I have come across fish there in other seasons as well.

False albacore lures and tackle are very similar to those used for bonito. The fish display a decided preference for flash. The Yo-Zuri Crystal Minnow and the Deadly Dick are still my two top lure choices for albies, and though I give the nod to the Crystal Minnow for bonito, I tend to favor the Deadly Dick for albies. Ironically, the real baitfish targeted by albacore are often a little chunkier. The main forage fish for albacore and other predators often shifts away the slender sand eels as the weather cools in the fall. The abundance of sand eels on the bonito bar drops off dramatically, and the fish's attention shifts to other baitfish leaving the harbors and estuaries, such as silversides. While they are very similar in appearance to sand eels, the silversides are slightly more bulky.

I have mentioned before that I believe fly fishing is very seldom the most effective way to catch a fish in saltwater. I love fly fishing, and I do it often, but not if my goal is simply to catch a fish. However, a possible exception to this may be fishing false albacore from a boat. In 2011, every false albacore I caught was on a fly rod. I was fly fishing at least ninety percent of the time, so that says very little. However, in my observations, fly fisherman around me were also enjoying more success than spin fisherman. This is an entirely unscientific observation, but it seemed that on my drifts out the Madaket cut this fall, the surrounding anglers with fly rods spent a lot time fighting fish, and those with spinning rods spent a lot of time feverishly reeling and scratching their heads. The same was true on my boat, and it seemed that even with my reduced casting range and the necessity of a few more seconds of casting to put a lure into breaking fish, I was enjoying more success with the fly. A fly put into breaking fish was rarely refused, whereas a lure put into the fish sometimes went through untouched.

Skok's Mushmouth remained the popular choice for the fall, and Mike caught most of his fish on one. I stuck with a bonito bunny with a little flash tied in, and I had excellent results. Two handed stripping, when you place the fly rod in your armpit and continuously strip in your line hand-over-hand is popular for albies, and bonito, but I much prefer traditional one-handed stripping. I make the longest strip I can as fast as I can, while remaining in control. The fly moves quickly enough to excite them, and I also find that a lot of strikes come when the fly is motionless in between strips.

False albacore will test your patience, and then they will test your tackle. They are an extremely popular fish these days, and with good reason. Anglers have also been very fortunate that there has been some good albacore fishing in the past several falls to make up, at least in part, for the lackluster striper fishing. Based on conversations with local fishermen with experience in more decades than myself, it seems that albies are playing a larger role in the fishing scene than ever before. This could be a good sign, pointing to healthy albie populations, large amounts of bait present in our waters in the fall, and more people paying attention to them as they gain popularity with the entire angling community. It could have negative connotations suggesting effects of global warming, and people just having to fish for something else because of lackluster fall striper fishing. Whatever the reason, they are an absolute blast, and the while they remain finicky and unpredictable, they are an excellent and rewarding fish to pursue.

CHAPTER FIVE

Bottom Fish

Rounding out Nantucket's inshore opportunities are bottom fish, namely fluke, black sea bass and scup. Both fluke (also known as summer flounder) and black sea bass are best known for their high culinary value, and most anglers pursuing them do so with an eye toward a tasty meal. Scup (or porgies) can be usually be found close to home and are targeted as table fare, live bait, and as a fairly easy and consistent target for beginners and youngsters to bend a rod.

Fluke

Fluke, or summer flounder, are perhaps the most prized of the inshore bottom fish. They grow to over twenty pounds, but specimens that big are rare. Any fish approaching ten pounds is a real beauty, and your average fish is two or three pounds.

The most consistent recreational fluking takes place along the eastern shore, south of Great Point to Sankaty, and more specifically from the waters east of Coskata south to the waters east of the Sankaty Beach Club. A large number of commercial draggers are often present in Nantucket Sound targeting fluke, but consistent action for recreational anglers is hard to come by (probably because of the draggers). The outer rips are also excellent places to find large fluke, and when the rips die out at slack tide, dropping bait and drifting over the edges slowly can be very productive.

Fluke, like other flounder, are a flatfish with both eyes on one side of their head, a camouflage back and a white belly. They lay in wait, blending seamlessly with the bottom, and when unsuspecting prey passes within range, they swiftly attack. Drifting bait along the bottom is the best way to target them. The best conditions to target fluke are when the wind and tide push you along in order to cover ground, but not so quickly that fishing the bottom becomes difficult. A drift of about two knots is perfect.

There are many different fluke rigs on the market, and they are easy and effective. They come with a snap for the weight, a swivel to attach to your main line, and a hook, or sometimes two, often bedazzled with some beads, spinner blades, or little rubber squid. Another very popular fluke rig is a bucktail or jig head and plastic of some kind, usually enhanced with a strip of bait, often with a teaser above it, usually also tipped with bait. The jig head or bucktail will act as the weight and the attractant and it should be fairly heavy: an ounce to three ounces depending on your depth and the wind and current.

The most common bait is squid. This is in no small part due to the fact it can be purchased in tackle shops and supermarkets and it is relatively inexpensive. It is also very effective. The best bait for fluke is fluke, as they are notoriously cannibalistic. In many states, using fluke for bait is illegal to discourage the practice of cutting up undersize specimens for use as bait, but the Massachusetts Fish and Game website lists fluke strips as an effective bait, and I can find no mention of it being prohibited in Massachusetts. Certainly, using an undersized specimen as the bait is illegal and filleting at sea without a special permit is also prohibited. When I fillet a fluke, I save the skins in a plastic bag, and freeze them for use on my next fluke trip. Both the white side and the brown-spotted side are effective as bait. In addition to being the best bait, they are also very durable and resilient. If you are on a multi-species trip, strips of the otherwise discarded belly-meat from bluefish or striped bass make good baits as well. The convenience and durability of the new wave of heavily scented soft artificial baits, such as the Berkley Gulp series, is also a consideration. These baits are just starting to pop onto the bottom-fishing scene here in the Northeast, but from what I have read and heard they are getting good results. Regardless of the bait you choose, cutting it into long thin strips is important. Rather than a glob of bait, you want a strip fluttering along seductively behind the hook.

Once you have dropped your offering to the bottom, slowly lift it and drop it. When you feel a bite, which will probably not be too subtle because when a fluke comes out of hiding, it does so quickly and violently, try to effectuate a short drop back before setting the hook. Fluke often need two bites to take in their prey. They will attack and grab the prey in their jaws, hold it there for a moment, and then open their jaws wide and suck in the entire thing with a second bite. If you try to set the hook hard on the first bite, the fluke may be just holding your bait in his jaws with the hook outside its mouth. By giving the fish a very short drop back, you let the fluke continue with their eating process and it is much more likely that your hook will be in the fluke's mouth when you set the hook. The drop back should be very short, and just dropping your rod tip toward the fish for a second after you feel the first bite is sufficient. Once you hook them, play them gently to the surface, and if they are near keeper-size and you are desirous of a meal, I would recommend keeping them in the water and netting them. They are adept at flipping themselves off hooks once they are lifted out of the water.

Off the eastern shore of the island, from fifteen feet out to forty can be productive, and depending on the wind and the tide, you will want to set your drift up to cover a good chunk of that water. The winds in the summer are predominantly southwest, and if that is the case, I would recommend starting your drift in fairly shallow water, around twenty feet, and drift east out to about thirty-five or forty feet. The tides along the eastern shore will push you either north or south. Depending on the success of your drift, you may want to change it or shorten it. For instance, you may find that on your drift from fifteen feet out to forty, that you got all the bites in between twenty-five and thirty feet of water, and in that case, replicate your drift, but only for the productive section. If your drift is totally unsuccessful, try moving north or south, and continue fishing different depths until you find something that is working.

Sand sharks, also known as dogfish, may be an issue when fluking or doing any bait fishing around the island. They are especially prevalent if you are fluking on the outer rips, but they are also a fair number of them along the eastern shore. The first issue they present is a safety one. If you catch a spiny dogfish, which you can identify by the small white spots on its back, they have a spike behind each fin on their back, and they will most certainly try to stab you with it. The spikes secrete a mild poison, and while not life threatening, if they get you, the wound will be very painful, prone to infection, and slow to heal. You may also catch a smooth dogfish, and it will not have white spots on its back or spikes behind its fins. Both species lack teeth despite being sharks. Smooth and spiny dogfish both put up a decent fight, and if bending the rod is a priority, sand sharks will fit the bill. Despite their toothlessness and their fairly small stature, they are unmistakably shark-like and that may be a source of excitement for youngsters or beginners. If you are looking for dinner, you may perhaps consider a sand shark. While seldom looked upon as food by American anglers, sand sharks are a popular food fish in other parts of the world (European fish and chips these days is often dogfish), and everybody I know who has eaten them has only good things to say. However, at times they can be thick and persistent, which may hamper your fluke efforts. If that is the case, you can change locations, or you can eliminate the bait. Sand sharks will seldom eat an artificial bait, and by leaving the bait off of your offering, and fishing just a plain artificial you can target the fluke exclusively. I have found Shimano's Lucanus Jigs and similar (much cheaper) options to be good choices for a plain artificial. This problem and solution is especially relevant when fluking the outer rips.

Due to their desirability as table fare, fluke are under extreme commercial pressure and tightly regulated. The regulations change too frequently to make printing them here helpful. But be aware of the regulations, both for size limits and bag limits as well as open and closed times of year. To add another wrinkle, regulations may differ for fluking in federal waters more than three miles offshore (the outer rips) and you will need to take that into consideration.

Black Sea Bass

Black sea bass are another bottom fishing option. The world record black sea bass is a hair over ten pounds, and the specimens you are likely to catch around Nantucket range from a couple ounces to a couple pounds, with some exceptionally big fish approaching five pounds being taken from time to time. They are extremely aggressive, and it is not uncommon when trolling wire-line at Sankaty to have one attack a parachute jig that is roughly its own size.

Sankaty is the best place to target black sea bass, and specifically, the Whale's Tail. Most charts of Sankaty will show a patch of water slightly shallower than the surround water protruding east from the beach and then widening in both directions, making the shape of a whale's tail, hence the name of the spot. The water rises from depths in the mid-thirties to the mid-twenties, and drifting over it usually produces consistent action with black sea bass. While the Whale's Tail is probably your best starting point, all of the waters off Sankaty can be productive, and as you move a little bit north of the light you get into some fluke territory and drifts in that area sometimes produce a mixed bag.

Much closer to home the wreck just north and west of the jetties holds sea bass as well. As far as I know, the wreck does not have a name and is known locally just as the wreck. It is more or less an open secret that in recent years the wreck has been growing in size, as some locals have taken what they perceive as a lack of structure around the island into their own hands, and a dive there would probably reveal some interesting items not onboard the original ship that went down. While I certainly have some reservations about unauthorized production of artificial structure, the fishing there gets better every year. Some nice big sea bass are taken there with some regularity, and you are likely to catch a mix of sea bass and scup.

While covering ground is often the ticket to good fluke fishing, staying pretty still is usually favorable for black sea bass. While at Sankaty you probably want to drift and cover some ground but a slow drift is favorable. While fishing on the wreck, you will probably do best anchoring once you located some fish, but be forewarned that losing an anchor in the structure is a distinct possibility, and that possibility gets more likely every season.

While I will sometimes use a convenient pre-tied "fluke rig" for fluke, I tie all my own sea bass rigs. I do this mainly because I like to fish circle hooks, usually size 1 or 1/0, for black sea bass. Usually when fishing for black sea bass, either at Sankaty or the wreck, you are going to catch a lot of small fish under the size limit and too small to eat even if it were legal. To help eliminate deep hooking the little guys I prefer circle hooks, and I find they are no less effective and easier to use than j-hooks. I usually use about four feet of thirty or forty-pound mono, and I will tie in one or two dropper loops for my circle hooks. I attach one end to my main line with a swivel and tie a loop in the bottom end large enough to fit through the eye and around the weight. I snug the loop back up on the eye of the weight, and the hooks are ready for bait. As with other circle hook applications, setting the hook is not recommended. When you feel a bite, just reel. Your hook-up ratio will be better than with j-hooks.

Squid is the best sea bass bait. While bluefish and striper belly strips are excellent for fluke, squid is a clear favorite of sea bass. Unlike the strip baits used for fluke, I prefer a big glob of bait for sea bass. Thread the hook through the squid several times, but be sure to leave the point of the hook exposed for good hook-ups. I like fishing with big baits, and I will often use a whole or half squid on one hook. I find that a big bait often attracts the big fish, and as I mentioned, trying to getting a big sea bass out of a crowd of little ones is a situation you are likely to find yourself in.

Just as in fluke fishing, sometimes you will find sand sharks around Sankaty, and sometimes when fishing the wreck you will find the scup more aggressive and numerous than you would like. In order to target strictly sea bass, get rid of the bait, just like fluke fishing. Drop a baitless offering to the bottom, a chrome Cripled Herring or other small flashy metal is good first choice, with a Lucanus or similar jig being a good option as well, and give it rapid bounces. Sea bass will happily hit an artificial and you will not be bothered by scup or sand sharks. While braided line is superior for all bottom fishing, it is particularly important with artificials to be able to impart the proper action.

Black sea bass are also subject to size and seasonal regulations that change frequently, so be sure to check them before you head out.

Scup

Scup are found primarily in and around the harbor. They are targeted successfully from piers and docks, they are plentiful in the anchorage and they are an increasingly popular target for anglers on Brant Point. The deep hole off Second Point is also a good place to find them, they are found around the ends of both jetties and they are plentiful on the wreck. On the west end, scup can be found around the bell buoy at the entrance of the channel and in the channel off Eel Point. They are particularly fond of structure.

Scup fishing is much like black sea bass fishing, only scaled down. Scup have very small mouths and to target them successfully, you should use small hooks baited with squid. I like to use the same rig I tie for black sea bass, except instead of size one circle, I use size three or four j-hooks. Being stationary or drifting very slowly is best for scup fishing. If you are in a boat, I would not advise you to be particularly patient. Scup are not likely to be traveling, and they probably will not smell your bait and move long distances to get it. If you drop your baits for a few minutes without any nibbles, I would head to a different spot.

Usually, around the harbor and on the wreck, you will not need a tremendous amount of weight to get your bait to the bottom, an ounce or less should get it done. The exception being Brant Point where the tide and depth necessitate more weight. Scup are small fish, a two pounder is real whopper, although the world record scup of over four pounds came from Nantucket Sound. If they are caught on light enough gear, they will put up a spirited fight. As table fare, they are not generally regarded as highly as fluke and black sea bass, but they are happily eaten by many. I will warn you that if you do intend on keeping a few for a meal, that they have a powerful and not necessarily appetizing odor when you filet them. This is normal, it dissipates upon cooking, and is not present in the flavor of the fish. As with other bottom fish, check the regulations before heading out.

CHAPTER SIX

Offshore

Nantucket is a great jumping-off point for offshore fishing, and while I will not offer too many specifics, I will point you in the right direction. As I discussed in the striped bass section regarding the offshore rips, the waters east of Nantucket are influenced by the cool Labrador Current, and the waters south of Nantucket are influenced by the Gulf Stream, and further south, rougly one hundred miles, you have the canyons and the Gulf Stream itself. This creates two different offshore environments, and you will need to decide whether to head east into the generally cooler water or south into the warm water. This decision will probably be based on what your target is, or in some cases, the desired size of the target.

East of the island you will find some of most famous and productive bluefin tuna grounds in the world. While some of the best giant bluefin fishing of the last few seasons has taken place more than a hundred miles offshore, most recreational fishing is done in the vicinity of thirty miles east of the island. Fishing for giants has been fairly lackluster in recent years, but there have been a few around, and east is where you will find the big boys. Fall is generally prime time for giants, but you never know when a fish of several hundred or even a thousand pounds may show up. Smaller bluefin are also present east of the island, and they have provided much more consistent action over the past several years. While live bait, chunking, and kites are often employed in pursuit of giants, recreational fishing for bluefin of all sizes is done primarily by trolling. Casting and jigging has become more practical primarily due to new superlines, and it is becoming more popular all the time. The most popular and effective trolled offerings are squid spreader bars and natural dead baits such as ballyhoo. More recently, soft plastics such as Hogys are being found in offshore spreads as well.

The tide is very important when fishing for tuna east of the island, but unlike most inshore fishing, the slack tide offers the best fishing. It is often the case that you will get bites during the slack tide, and the rest of the day will yield nothing. If fishing is good all day, it will probably be exceptional on the slack tide. First light is also an excellent time to get bites, though keep in mind when scheduling your trip that if the sun rises around 5:30 on Nantucket, which is a good average for the summer, and you want to be thirty miles east of Nantucket with lines in the water thirty minutes or so before that, you are looking at a very early departure time and some running in the dark.

Offshore bottom fishing also takes place east of the island, with codfish being the main target. The good spots for tuna are often the good spots for cod, and a number of both can be found in the vicinity, and it is certainly possible to combine them on a day fishing east.

Another good aspect about fishing to the east is that you are very likely to see humpback and other species of whales. They frequent the same waters, and they are actually a very good sign. Often the whales and the tuna will be in the same waters. While the tuna fishing is certainly hit or miss, the whales are more consistent. It is not unusual to see fifty or more whales if visibility is good (it is often foggy) and they are usually fun to watch. They breech, fluke, splash and show their tales.

Lastly, sharks are found east, usually very big sharks. The vast majority of recreational shark fishing takes place in the warmer waters to the south of the island, but sometimes during the Vineyard or Nantucket shark tournaments, anglers will head east in search of very big fish. This was last successful in 2010 when Captain Jay Starr went about twenty-five miles east brought in a 353lbs. mako during the Nantucket Shark Tournament. However, if you are recreationally pursuing sharks, I would recommend heading south.

Most shark fishing takes place between fifteen miles and thirty miles south or southwest. Sharks are obviously found much further out, but running any more than thirty miles is usually unnecessary. Shark fishing is done by stopping your boat and setting out a chum line. Chum is ground up oily fish, usually menhaden when store bought or bluefish when homemade, and the easiest (and cleanest) way to create your chum line it is to freeze it and then place it overboard in a durable bucket with holes in it and let it melt and naturally disperse. Sharks have an extremely acute sense of smell and once they get a whiff of the chum, they will follow it right to your boat.

Use large single hooks baited with bluefish chunks, mackeral, or any other fish, and rigged on stiff wire leaders six to ten feet. I usually set out three baits, one on the surface, one near the bottom, and one in the middle. For the two deep baits, I make my own heavy-duty inline sinkers by threading several hundred pound monofilament through an egg sinker of several ounces, and crimp a snap swivel on one end to attach the leader, and a loop on the other end to clip into the snap swivel at the end of the main line. This way, I can change the sinker fairly effortlessly between rods and it lasts a few seasons. Tie a balloon onto the line when the bait has reached your desired depth and then let the balloon drift away from the boat. Snugging a rubber band around the line behind the balloon should keep it from slipping up the line. Much like pond fishing with a bobber, when your balloon gets pulled under or starts racing across the surface, start cranking and set the hook when it comes tight.

Makos and thresher sharks are the top targets in shark fishing. Makos are odd in that sometimes one will fight very little, and come to the boat almost without objection, and other times, they will put on a show like no other fish in the sea. There is no clear answer to what the fastest fish in the sea is, Atlantic sailfish get the nod most of the time, but makos, along with bluefin tuna and wahoo often get tossed into the debate. Regardless of whether or not makos are the fastest fish in the sea, they can really scream and they are capable of some amazing jumps. They will not take to the air as early or often as billfish or tarpon and they usually do not make a succession of jumps, but they will fly high. They often come to the surface at full speed from a significant depth, and they do not slow at all upon reaching the surface. I have had hooked makos go at least fifteen feet in the air, and they are capable of going thirty feet. This is something to keep in mind when fighting a mako, and you do not want to bring it close until both you and the fish are ready. Threshers also jump occasionally, but they are more likely to make some impressive runs and then stubbornly battle to the end.

Both makos and threshers are good to eat, although most people agree that their quality as a food fish decreases in reverse proportion to their size. Makos around the hundred pound mark are delicious and their flesh is extremely similar to swordfish. I have eaten fish around 170lbs that I still found delicious, but as they eclipse the two hundred pound mark the meat starts to take on an acrid tinge. If you can bring yourself to forgo the dock-side victory photos, you should consider releasing any huge sharks, both because their value as a meal will be marginal, and because killing a shark that big will be no easy task.

The sharks you are most likely to come across are blue sharks. Their greatest attribute is their consistency. When you go offshore and start a chum line, even on a slow day you can usually count on a few blue sharks seeking you out. They usually do not hesitate to eat a hook-bait and they can grow very large. It is not uncommon to catch specimens ten feet or longer. They have neither the speed nor leaping ability of the mako, but they will pull very hard and they have stamina. My chief complaint is that they have the very unappealing habit of spending large chunks of the fight right under your boat. This is tough place to get them to budge from, and it tends to bend expensive offshore rods at extreme angles that may break them. Blue sharks sometimes set upon you in numbers, and congregate around your chum bucket, and if you are after a mako or a thresher, this can make keeping a bait in the water difficult. If this is the case, you can do one of four things. The first being send your bait or baits deep and far. Distract the blue sharks with little chunks of bluefish tossed away from one side of the boat and on the other side of the boat, get a bait sunk deep past them, and then sent out on a balloon. There is still a pretty good shot a blue shark will track down your bait, but it will certainly last longer than if you try to send one out on the surface. The next option is to continue chumming, but pull all of your baits out of the water, and only put one back in when a mako or a thresher is spotted or when the blue sharks leave. Another option is to keep catching blue shark after blue shark, usually with some of the same ones working their way back into the rotation shortly after being released (they seem either very quick to forgive and trust again, or to have a very short memory). Some captains are of the mind that the constant commotion of catching will add to the appeal of the chum line and get the attention of more sharks. The last option and one I have had a lot of success with is to put out a ballyhoo on a hook. I have had blue sharks eat ballyhoo and I have had makos swim by a ballyhoo in favor of piece of bluefish, but both in my experience, are the exception rather than the rule. On more than one occasion I have had blue sharks swimming around my chum bucket and transom for extended periods of time while a ballyhoo under a balloon has remained unmolested in the chum slick until a mako showed up.

I have also become fond of continuing to catch sharks, though not in the traditional way. Rather than continue to catch big blues on heavy offshore conventional tackle, I will rig big light-wire circle hooks and leaders of three or four feet on twenty pound class spinning rods and purposely target the smaller blue sharks. Wrestling a three-hundred pounder out from under the boat is something I never want to do again, and something my clients rarely want to do more than once, but battling the thirty to eighty pounders on light gear is a lot of fun. If they do dive under the boat, maneuvering them out is easy enough with the versatile and mobile spinning gear, and releasing the fish is a snap, I just grab the leader and the hook straightens and pops right out, and the shark swims away (usually for at least for a minute or two).

You can also head south to troll for a mixed bag. There is consistent world class action in the canyons, which are roughly one hundred miles south. This is where the continental shelf ends, and water depths plummet from a few hundred feet to a few thousand, and the Gulfstream is there, pumping warm water into the shelf. By consistent fishing, I do not mean that driving a hundred miles south and putting your lines in the water is going to yield a big day every time. I mean that there are fish there from roughly July through September and they are likely to be biting somewhere. There are several canyons and a few hundred square miles of water, and one hundred miles offshore is quite a big undertaking, not to mention expensive, so be sure to do as much research as possible to ensure you arrive at a lively area.

For more accessible action, warm water eddies from the Gulfstream often push up over the continental shelf and come within easy day trip range of Nantucket, with good offshore action occasionally taking place within ten miles. Bluefin tuna are also found south of Nantucket, and they are almost exclusively juveniles, usually fifteen to fifty pounds. There was a good small bluefin bite between six and ten miles out in July of 2011. Yellowfin tuna are also found south of island, and if a really warm eddy spins up with water temperatures in the mid seventies, that is the place to look for yellowfin. Dolphinfish, known also as mahi-mahi or dorado, and are probably the most consistent of the warm water offshore species other than sharks. Dolphin love flotsam, and if you are offshore in water temperatures of about seventy or above and you find a floating piece of debris, it is likely to have dolphin under it that are usually quite happy to take a hook baited with squid or a ballyhoo chunk. The dolphin south of Nantucket tend to be small, especially the ones congregating on flotsam, but I have trolled up some nice size fish in the thirty pound class south of the island. If you find flotsam with a lot of small dolphin, try using a weighted rig to get a chunk of bait below them. Often some larger fish will be hanging out a little deeper or on the outskirts.

South of Nantucket used to be a prime spot to find white marlin, and in particular to sight them tailing and cast to them. The last truly good year was 1998; whites were everywhere. The boats in the *Nantucket Anglers' Club Billfish Tournament* that year broke all the previous white marlin release records, with one boat catching ten in a day. It was the year before I started running the *Topspin*, and my offshore capabilities and experience were non-existent. I had plans to fish with Uncle Bob and a friend one day, but they were cancelled by weather, the bite came to a close, and I headed off to college. I have maintained high hopes of a return every since, over what has been a decade and change of very bleak white marlin fishing. White marlin are hit very hard by long-liners, and their populations have plummeted. From 1999 to 2009, finding a white marlin anywhere short of the canyons was a long shot. However, there is reason for cautious optimism. In 2010, I heard a few reports of people seeing white marlin short of the canyons, and in 2011, there were a lot of the reports. My own white marlin hysteria was in full force for a few weeks in August that I had some offshore trips scheduled. We were primarily sharking, but I saw several whites. I baited one particularly unhungry fish about five times without success. A few days later we finally got one to eat, we were trolling and it came into the spread and we pitched him a ballyhoo rigged on a circle hook. He ate and we dropped it back, and then came tight on him, and I could not have scripted a better scenario for a solid hook-up. He screamed off on a run, and then flew out of the water and shook his head, and the hook shot back at us like it came out of a slingshot. Ninety-nine times out of hundred, the hook would have found its way into the corner of the fishes mouth, but on this occasion, I believe the fish had his jaw shut so tightly on the leader that the hook just laid benignly in its mouth until it jumped, and then it just flew back at us. That is as close to catching a marlin as I have ever been, and if you are looking for more in-depth information on how to catch them, I will let you read about it from somebody whose experience amounts to more than a few encounters culminating in one supremely heartbreaking lost fish. Hopefully, the marlin appearances of 2011 are a sign of good things` to come, and I will not have to wait another twelve years for another shot.

With skipjack tuna sometimes present and the very occasional wahoo being reported recently, that rounds out the species you are likely to find in the waters short of the canyons, and if you make the trek all the way out to them, add albacore tuna, bigeye tuna, blue marlin and swordfish to the list.

Regardless of what direction you are headed and what species your are targeting, be sure to prepare properly for your trip. First and foremost this means checking the weather, making sure your safety equipment is present and in good shape, and doing everything you can to make sure your boat is ready. You may not be alone offshore, but you need to assume you will be, and you need to be prepared.

Once you have taken appropriate safety measures, gather all of the information you can to try and arrive at a lively patch of water. Gather fishing reports, the more current the better, and take a look at ocean temperature charts. If you are going offshore on a regular basis, you should consider subscribing to an offshore fishing service, such as Roffers or Terrafin, that will provide you will current ocean temperatures and fishing information. One of the major factors in locating fish offshore is water temperature, and with today's technology, you can get a pretty accurate picture of that before you leave the dock, or if you have the latest technology, you can get a picture of it on your boat's electronics. Generally speaking, you want to fish where some hot water meets some cold water. Well defined breaks in temperature tend to concentrate bait and attract fish. If there is some seventy-three degree water coming up from the south and bumping into a patch of sixty-seven degree water to its northeast, right where they meet is a good place to start. In an absolute best-case scenario, there would be bluefin tuna in the cool and yellowfin tuna and dolphin in the hot, with the possibility of a white marlin on both sides. Temperature breaks are also good places to begin your chum slick in search of sharks, with most anglers favoring the cool side for makos and threshers.

The next thing to look for is life. Once you get offshore, it is a big ocean, and many times it is going to offer you very little in the way of clues on where the fish are. Any kind of life is a good sign and the more the better. If you are east, the tuna are likely to be around the whales, birds and dolphins. If you are south whales are much less likely but keep your eye out for birds, baitfish of any kind, dolphins (the mammals), and sharks cruising the surface (even if they are not your target). Life is found in patches offshore, and where any life is found, there are usually exchanges happening up and down the food chain.

CHAPTER SEVEN

Tackle and Rigging

An important step in your fishing adventure is going to be your trip to the tackle store. If you are familiar with your tactics and quarry and you have money in your pocket, you may be as joyous as the proverbial kid in the candy store, with so many fancy toys and tools all laid out before you. However, tackle these days is fairly complicated and if you are new to the sport, the intended species or the area, a tackle store may be quite daunting. Having spent a little time behind the counter at tackle shops, I have seen this from time to time, and usually when the potential angler's objectives are narrowed, then the rod and reel choice becomes manageable. From time to time you also get someone who dismisses the varied selection and distinctions and declares something like, "I just need a regular fishing rod," which is like going to a car dealership and saying you just need a regular car. You may drive out into the New England winter in your new convertible, or you may end up trying to tow your boat with a sensible compact. There is no rod or reel that does it all. As is the case with most specialization, the more particularly suited your rod and reel is to one type of fishing, the less versatility it is going to have.

The first question to ask yourself is what kind of fishing you are going to do? Are you going to be primarily casting or trolling? Are you going to be fishing from a boat or the beach, or both? Are you going to be fishing at

Sankaty or on the flats? Once you have figured out what kind of fishing you are going to be doing, then you can seriously start to narrow your options. If you are only going to be doing one kind of fishing, then your choice of setup is pretty easy. It becomes tougher when you want to do a few different things, and you have to consider whether you want the best possible setup for each different circumstance, or whether space, simplicity, money and, probably not least of all, your spouse, dictate that you get a more versatile setup that can perform a variety of fishing tasks rather than a myriad of specialized setups.

Spinning Rods

Unless you plan to troll and bottom fish exclusively, the place to start is a spinning set up, and more specifically the rod.

The first standard question of the past was whether you would be primarily fishing from the beach or from a boat, and that dictated the length of your rod: longer rods for longer casts from the beach, and shorter, more manageable lengths for the boat. That is a consideration, certainly. If you plan on doing most of your fishing on the south shore, Great Point, or any big water, you do not want a little six-footer and if you are on a boat a twelve-footer is going to be difficult, both to fish with and transport, and perhaps dangerous. However, I am not sure it should be the first question anymore. For instance, if you plan on doing most of your fishing around the harbors in shallow water near inlets and flats, the aforementioned twelve-footer is going to be as equally out of place there as it is on a boat and you are going to want a shorter, lighter rod.

It may seem like putting the cart before the horse, but it is prudent to consider what type of lure you will be using the most, and then select the appropriate rod. In an extreme case, a long light rod that does well flinging small unweighted soft plastics is probably going to snap like an expensive twig if you try to throw a Hopkins or Ballistic Missile with it. Rods are manufactured with the recommended lure-weight printed right on them, and making sure that coincides with the lures you plan to throw is a consideration. Keep in mind that if a rod claims to cast everything from ¼ of an ounce to 5 ounces, it probably casts nothing well, and while a rod designed to throw lures of ½ to ¾ of an ounce is pretty limited, it probably casts those lures like a dream. If you fish from the beach, but you do it mostly in the harbors and tranquil water, you will probably want a very light rod around seven feet, and the same rod would be very well suited to fishing the flats in a boat. Figuring out where and with what you are going to fish is a more applicable determination that just contemplating beach vs. boat.

Notwithstanding the importance I have placed on the differences in rods and reels, I have a handful of fairly versatile rods and they see the bulk of my light-tackle action all summer. I fish rods of about seven feet in length and rated for lures between ½ to 1½ ounces. I use these set-ups on the beaches, on the flats, they are perfect for east-tide Great Point stripers, and they are my bonito and false albacore rods. These rods also reflect my own favorites in terms of methods and lures. They are not particularly well suited to surf fishing, except in protected and tranquil waters, they are not capable of throwing heavy lures, my bonito bar staple, the sinking Yo-Zuri Crystal Minnow weighs in at one ounce and that is near the top of their capabilities.

The exception to these versatile rods, given my own preference for unweighted soft plastics and the fact that I need to own a great deal of rods for the use of clients, is that I have a 7½ -foot beauty that is very light and rated for lures from 3/8 to ¾ of an ounce. It is my best performing rod for throwing unweighted plastics, but the downside is that it is too light even for the one ounce Yo-Zuris, and it usually spends bonito and false albacore season on the bench.

Going up a little bit in size, not necessarily in length but in the recommended lure weight, is also a very versatile choice. The bulk of the spinning set-ups on *Topspin* fit this mold. They are six or seven feet, and capable of throwing lures to three ounces. They are great for fishing the Old Man and other deep water rips with Bombers for stripers, they are perfect for casting Ballistic Missiles and other heavy lures to bluefish. It will also be an effective live-bait rod. While a conventional rod and reel is a better bet for consistent trollers, spinning rods of this class can be trolled with no problem. They are also excellent choices for bottom fishing. It is a common mistake for people to associate smaller rods and gear with bottom fishing because the fish are smaller, but you want a fairly stout set-up for bottom fishing, especially east of the island. You need of rod capable of handling the necessary weight, and a stiff rod is also very helpful in bottom fishing to be able to feel the bottom and subtle bites and to quickly and effectively set the hook. Extending the length of the rod, to perhaps ten to twelve feet, and keeping the same lure weight recommendations and reel is a good choice for a traditional surf rod, and something around eight feet offers a compromise for both beach and boat duty.

Once you have made your choice as to how heavy and how long you want, then it is a matter of selecting one that fits your criteria that is in your price range. You can spend $25 to $1,000, and just about anything in between. A wonderful development in recent years is that the lifetime warranty is becoming more common and available even on mid-priced rods. A few rods around the hundred dollar mark, and many under two hundred now come with a lifetime warranty, and the biggest piece of advice I have in regards to choosing your brand is that you consider one with a lifetime warranty. Fishing rods are innately delicate and you are likely to break one once in while, sometimes fishing and sometimes not. In either case, over time, your warranty is going to save you a lot of money. Also inquire as to the warranty process: some tackle shops and manufactures let you walk in with your broken rod and walk out with a new one off the shelf, some require you to mail the rod back to them, which can be fine, and some make you mail the rod back to them with an included "fee," which if you ask me is not much of a lifetime warranty at all. Some manufactures are very happy to replace rods and offer no fault and no questions asked warranties. Others may inspect the rod and question you to determine whether the rod broke playing a fish with otherwise appropriate tackle or whether you slammed it in your car door, to avoid giving you another rod when possible.

Spinning Reels

I have had a lot of reels from a lot of manufacturers over the years, and I have been both delighted and supremely disappointed with most of them. I now favor Daiwa reels, for both function and value. It has largely been my experience that you generally get what you pay for, and for a reel with a smooth drag that will last quite a while, you are probably looking at between one hundred and two hundred dollars. In the last few years there has been a proliferation of spinning reels on the market that approach or even eclipse the thousand dollar price tag. I have never fished one, and I do not foresee a day in the future when I will purchase one. Most of my brain agrees that paying that much for a spinning reel is ludicrous, but I would be lying if said I was not curious about how awesome they really are. I believe a handful of these super-high end reels have lifetime warranties, and I would love to see that trend work its way to the mid-range price models as it has with rods.

Factors other than price to consider are balance and line capacity. Once you have selected your rod, try the reels out on it. Make sure they feel and look right are not too heavy or too light. If you are a beginner, the tackle store clerk should be able to help you out with this. Consider how much line your reel needs to hold. It is rare to find a reel that holds less than two hundred yards of the appropriate line, and it rare to find an inshore fish for which you would need more than two hundred yards of line. Although you may find fish that can push those limits, false albacore and very large stripers come to mind, and those are the fish your really do not want to lose. Casting and the use of spinning rods offshore is becoming more and more popular, and if you plan on enlisting your reel in some offshore duty, line capacity quickly becomes a priority. Tuna, marlin and sharks can dump two hundred yards of line off your reel in seconds, and having a reel capable of holding at least double that is a good idea.

Conventional Rods and Reels

Conventional rods and reels are your best option for offshore trolling, with rods and reels from the 50# to 130# class the norm for east of the island and 30# to 50# being more suitable south of the island until you reach the canyons when some of the heavier stuff will come back into play. Closer to home conventional setups can be used for trolling both in open water and in rips and for bait fishing and bottom fishing as well, but for inshore use, they lack the versatility of spinning rods.

If you plan to do any wire-line fishing at all, you will need setups dedicated only to wire-lining and they will not be serviceable for any other types of fishing without some fairly significant changes. A wire-line set-up is as specialized as it gets. You will need a large conventional reel and a very stout rod that is specifically designed for wire-line. Wire-line will quickly dig grooves into the inside of your rod guides if they are not specifically designed for wire. The line will wear and catch on these grooves and your rod will be useless for both wire and non-wire. Once you have the appropriate rod and reel, load it with Dacron backing, wire, and a leader as discussed in the section on fishing wire-line.

Line

I have made the transition from mono to braid, and now I fish it on almost all of my spinning rods. I like more line capacity, increased casting distance, durability, and no stretch. Although braided line is significantly more expensive, it is said to retain its full breaking strength for twenty years, whereas if a reel full of mono lasts one full season it is a rarity. The trouble with this, of course, is it does not matter how long the braided line will last if it is in a very expensive, unmanageable bird's nest that needs to be cut. Unfortunately, especially if you are new to braid, that is sure to happen, but it can be minimized. Certainly avoid the usual causes of bird nests: overfilling the spool, reeling against the drag, and retrieves or lures that cause line-twisting.

Additionally, I have a lot of luck manually flipping the bail over after my cast and before my retrieve, instead of just starting my retrieve. My first casts in saltwater were throwing big poppers for bluefish on stout rods and Penn reels. To maximize your lure's time splashing around, starting your retrieve immediately when your lure hit the water was best, and I learned to cast, and then start cranking immediately when my lure hit the water. The bail flipped automatically, and that was that. I had to get out of the habit of letting my first cranks flip the bail automatically, and do it by hand. By letting the bail flip with the cranking of the reel, you impart a few twists into the line each time, and sometimes lay a little loose line on the spool, both of which will play a role in creating tangles. In addition to avoiding tangles in braid, I am told that flipping the bail by hand is actually much better for today's lighter, smoother, and more delicate reels.

If a bird's nest does occur, unlike mono, your line may still be salvageable. If you can untangle the braid, it has no memory, so it will not immediately tangle again like mono would. If you are in a position to take your time and slowly pick the tangle apart, you will probably be able to save your line. Having another rod on hand is nice, in case the fishing is good (or you think it may start to get good soon) and you don't have the time to pick at your line. You can just stow the rod with a bird nest and take your time untangling your line at home later. After an appropriate time loosening and trying to untangle your bird's nest, (only you will be able to determine what is an appropriate amount of time when trying to save about $30 worth of line), if you are left with a knot, just pull both ends, preferably with gloves as braid can slice through your hand pretty easily, and sometimes you'll get lucky and the knot will pull out.

I rig my spinning rods in pretty much the same manner for the early season south shore stripers, light-tackle casting in the harbors, flats fishing and bonito and false albacore fishing. I spool the reel with 15lbs. or 20lbs. braid. Since the advent of braid, I know a lot of anglers have started using heavier breaking strengths. Thirty or even forty pound braid still has plenty of feel and castability, and it is thin enough that your reel will have plenty of line on it. All of these seem like valid reasons to me, and if you want to spool up with braid that has a similar diameter to your old mono rather than breaking strength, or some compromise in between, that is effective. Personally though, I prefer to stick with 15lbs. or 20lbs. I like the increased feel, the longer casts, and the increased capacity that the smaller line provides. It is also a distinct possibility that I merely just prefer the idea of fishing with line with a stated breaking strength of something less than the weight of the fish I may actually catch.

Regardless of what type of line you are using, by and large Nantucket is not a place where you need to be concerned about a fish running into structure and breaking you off. This is a chief concern in many locales: if you are snook fishing among mangroves for instance, if a hooked fish is able to run into the mangroves, which it will almost certainly try very hard to do, it is all but impossible to get him back out, and it will probably break you off. Bottom fishing where a grouper or snapper is able to get back into a hole in a reef or wreck is another scenario where the angler will usually not win. Those types of fishing call for fairly heavy tackle because immediately when the fish is hooked it needs to be stopped before it goes too far. When fishing around Nantucket, it is generally fine to let the fish run where it wants and tire itself out a little bit, and you do not need to worry about vegetation, rocks or reefs. The only possible exceptions would be fishing with extremely light tackle in heavy grass and the moorings and lobster pots present in parts of the harbor and around Tuckernuck. Especially in parts of Madaket harbor, the eel grass can grow fairly tall and hooked fish will often burrow through it, and a large amount can end up on your line. The 15lbs. I use is usually enough to work the fish out of the grass, or work both the fish and grass to the boat, but if you were are using lighter line, the grass could create a problem. Aside from switching to heavier tackle or fishing a location with less grass, there is no solution. Not every fish will burrow through the grass, and if you want to fish 8lbs. test and stripers are biting in a grassy area, the threat of a fish breaking you off in the grass shouldn't be enough to deter you, but it is something to be aware of. If you are fishing in close proximity to moorings or lobster pots, then you may consider beefing up your tackle a little bit to keep the fish out of them.

Braided line is a tremendous advantage bottom fishing. The thinner diameter reduces the effect of the tide and currents on your line, making it much easier to get to the bottom and stay there without having to use excess weight. It also makes it much easier to feel when you are on the bottom and it transmits nibbles and bites much better, leading to more hookups.

Braided line is also becoming more and more common offshore, and the increased strength and line capacity it can provide is largely what is driving the increased feasibility and popularity of offshore casting. On conventional trolling rods, its increased capacity is a tremendous advantage, and if you are inclined, it can allow you to scale down your gear. However, when trolling offshore, the stretch inherent in monofilament is a necessary factor in tempering the savage strikes, runs and jumps of offshore fish. To get the best of both worlds, fill your reel with braided line most of the way, and then add a section of monofilament, known as a top shot and usually between twenty-five and one hundred yards, on top of the braided line. The monofilament section will stretch and yield and offer some forgiveness through the fight, and you will still have the increased strength and capacity of braid.

In addition to a propensity for bird nests, braided line is also difficult to knot and to cut. Having a pair of scissors is your best bet for cutting it, and while there are several models of expensive "braided line scissors" on the market, I have been happy using regular scissors or very cheap "braided line scissors". Another drawback to braided line is that it is not transparent like mono, and it is visible in the water. While I would seldom recommend fishing straight mono to your lure, a leader becomes a necessity with braid. For my light tackle rods, I usually tie a section of fluorocarbon, usually about three feet of 25lbs, to the braided main line with a double uni-knot.

For the larger spinning rods onboard *Topspin*, I usually spool them with 30 or 40lbs. braid, and I tie a Bimini twist in the braid and connect that to a snap swivel via an offshore swivel knot. The lures we may use are already rigged with the appropriate leaders with a perfection loop in the end, and we just clip the loop onto the snap swivel. This makes for very quick and easy lure changes, and it keeps the terminal tackle away from the lure.

Fly Tackle

Ironically, in an arena of fishing that is full of infinite variations and subleties in tackle, I currently do all of my fly fishing with an eight weight, and while I own sinking lines, I use my floating line about ninety-five percent of the time. I think that I am probably in the minority in that most anglers probably regard a slow or intermediate sinking line as the most versatile for striper fishing, and most of the lines you see marketed as "striped bass fly lines" are just that. In my opinion a floating line is more versatile and much better suited to the fly fishing around the island. Most of my fly fishing takes place on the flats in depths where anything except a floating line just would not make sense. I can still fish down in the water column a little bit just by using a Clouser or other weighted pattern. A floating line works well at Great Point, but if you plan on fishing some of the deeper rips on the fly, certainly a sinking line would be more consistently effective. I have always enjoyed the most success at the Bonito Bar on a floating line, but that is partially do to my own preference for using one, and I would imagine that an intermediate sinking line would also be very effective. When chasing busting albies, not only will a floating line keep your offering in the midst of the feeding, but it will also make it easier to pick up your line and shoot it back into the fray, although I do not think a intermediate sinking line would be much of handicap in that situation either.

I like the eight-weight very much, and if you are looking for your first fly rod, I think an eight-weight is perfectly suited to Nantucket. I think many Northeast fly anglers may recommend a bigger outfit, a nine or ten-weight, but I prefer the eight-weight for Nantucket. The first consideration is the bait. The big baitfish, most notably bunker, that are found in other parts of the Northeast make only rare appearances around Nantucket. What we do have is sand eels, in abundance. Most of the time, you are going to be throwing little sand eel imitations rather than trying to heave out a large profile fly, and you do not want or need a particularly stout fly rod to do it. The exception being fishing the big water rips, probably with a large squid fly and perhaps sinking line, and this pushes an eight-weight to the limit. Through an unplanned set of circumstances, I currently own three eight weights, but I am vaguely in the market for a ten weight for big water rips and a twelve or thirteen weight for tuna and other offshore pursuits that I hope will also serve me well in pursuit of Florida tarpon.

I would recommend you look into both rods and reels from Temple Fork Outfitters. In the world of fly tackle, some of the price tags are high enough to inspire laughter, confusion or disbelief, and TFO makes and sells very nice rods, with lifetime warranties and excellent customer service, for a fraction of what similar quality rods go for.

Once you have selected a rod, find a reel to match. You are going to want at least a couple hundred yards of backing and your appropriate line, but pretty much every reel you find is going to provide that. Prices are going to range from less than one hundred to well over thousand. As with rods, I am have been very pleased with TFO reels and they are generally at the lower end of the price-range. I have a Tibor Everglades that my wonderful wife gave me as a wedding present, which is fantastic. It has a smooth, world-class drag and it is solid and durable, yet lightweight. It is a beautiful satin gold, and has my name and a striped bass engraved on it, and I admit those certainly add to its allure.

For fly leaders I generally tie my own three or four part fluorocarbon leaders tapered from a thirty or thirty-five pound butt section down to a ten or fifteen pound tippet. Of the myriad of gadgets that go along with fly-fishing, one I would recommend is a stripping basket. I much prefer fishing without one than with one, but whether you are fishing from the beach, wading, or from a boat, you will find times when one is necessary. If you are beach fishing, you may want to cover some ground and dragging your line around behind you is going to cause problems, if you are wading, the current may be swift enough that leaving your line in the water is going to hamper your casting, and you may find yourself on a boat that has a lot of things to catch a fly line.

Sunglasses

The last piece of equipment you are going to need is polarized sunglasses, and they should be a priority. In middle school when I started reading all of the fishing literature I could get my hands on, I questioned whether polarized sunglasses were as important as my reading suggested, and I doubted that a simple pair of sunglasses could make the difference between being able to see and not see the fish. Now that I have a great deal of experience looking for fish, I assure you I was wrong, and the effects of polarized sunglasses are phenomenal.

For any kind of fishing that seeing the fish is necessary or advantageous, they are an essential. I do not have the faintest idea how they work, but they cut a huge percentage of the glare off the surface of the water, making it possible to see much deeper and with much more clarity than would be possible without them. When I am sight fishing for stripers at Great Point, I can see the individual fish in the waves very clearly much of the time, yet the fish remain invisible even when I point them out to customers without polarized glasses. I will give them a pair of polarized glasses, and they can immediately see the fish and are amazed.

Even if you do not plan to sight fish, I would not recommend going fishing without them. You never know when an opportunity may present itself, and there is nothing to lose by being able to see further and more clearly into the water. You will be able to see bait, vegetation and weeds, water color and clarity and perhaps the bottom much better, and that can never hurt.

Polarized glasses also have a tremendous price range, with some available for around twenty bucks and some pairs costing well over two hundred. I have worn pretty high-end Costa Del Mars for years, and I am very pleased with them. I think their clarity is impressive, and they claim that you will be able to see fish further under the water than with any other glasses. While I haven't tested this or anything, I really have no reason to doubt it and I have seen some fish that were pretty far under the surface. If you are going to fish often, I would recommend an expensive pair, but a cheap option will probably be serviceable if you are not going to use them often, or you are prone to losing a lot of sunglasses. One thing to consider is that they are perfectly good sunglasses for everyday use as well, and while I think Costa Del Mar largely targets the fishing crowd, there is no reason not to make them your everyday sunglasses, and in that regard, they may become your most-used piece of fishing tackle.

CHAPTER EIGHT

Choosing the Right Captain or Guide

As I mentioned in the introduction, hiring a local guide is an excellent way to get started fishing around Nantucket, and I would highly recommend it. Reading this book is one thing, but having an experienced professional take you to the fish and show you how to catch them is a service that cannot be replicated with just words.

You may want to consider chartering a boat more often even if you are not new to angling or Nantucket (or anywhere else). While guided fishing is not cheap, compared to boat ownership, it is an absolute bargain. If you are considering buying a boat, I recommend you look at chartering a boat as many times as you want instead. When you look at the expenses of buying and maintaining a boat, fueling it up, buying tackle, and other incidentals, you are talking about thousands up front (probably tens or hundreds of thousands depending on the boat), and thousands more each year on upkeep. You can go fishing with a professional on their boat many, many times over the course of a season for much less money and never have to worry about maintenance, tackle, dockage, winter storage, or anything. You show up, fish, and head home. You do not even have to clean the boat or fillet your own fish. Even if you are a skilled and experienced angler, if you choose the right captain they are going to have their finger on the pulse of the fishing and be able to consistently get you into good action. I see this reality more and more all the time. Many of my customers are local or summer residents of the island, they are competent anglers, and having their own boat is a possibility. It is just far cheaper and much easier to go with me, and for the money they save by not owning a boat, they can fish with me virtually as much as they want and still come out way ahead.

But, just finding a captain and hiring him is most certainly not the way to ensure a good trip that meets your expectations. I am the first to admit that guided fishing is not cheap, and you want to do everything you can to ensure your trip is a success. Obviously there are going to be a number of conditions outside the control of you or your guide, but doing the proper research and preparation can certainly put the odds in your favor.

The advice I offer here is garnered from extensive experience as both the captain and the customer. Even though I am a very experienced angler, I understand the importance of local knowledge, and when I go someplace new, I always try to fish with a guide at least once. The ways to go about finding a good match as far a captain or guide and the ways to stack the odds in your favor are fairly universal, and while I illuminate some local subtleties, I recommend you follow this advice when arranging guided fishing anywhere, not just Nantucket.

The first thing to do is plan ahead. While this is not always necessary, and you will usually be able to find somebody to take you fishing even on short notice, the best captains during the best times and tides are the first to get booked and if you wait until the last minute, there is a distinct possibility you will not be choosing from the cream of the crop.

The next thing to do is communicate with your prospective captain, and this goes hand in hand with planning ahead. If you call a Nantucket charter boat captain in August, and you want to discuss your fishing options at length, what tackle they provide and what they intend to use, what the target species will be, what other species are available, what time is the best time to go, etc., you may have the best intentions and they may be the nicest guy in the world, but they just may not have the time to discuss it all with you. They will probably have been fishing ten to fourteen hours a day for several weeks straight, the best times to go are already booked anyway, and they just need to get some sleep. On the other hand, if you give them a call or shoot them an email in March or April, they would probably be very happy to chat for a while about the different options likely to be available during the time of your trip, they will be able to give you a pretty clear picture of what to expect, and you will have your choice of the best times and tides.

If you are planning your trip around fishing, the previous sections of this book should give you an excellent idea of when to plan your trip, but contact your prospective captain or captains and get their thoughts as well. Certainly one of the best things you can do to stack the odds in your favor is to come to Nantucket during the absolute best time to do whatever it is you want to do, such as coming in June to fish for stripers, August to fish for bonito or offshore, and September for false albacore.

On the other hand, in my experience it is probably more likely that your trip to Nantucket has been scheduled around work, vacation, family or some reason other than to coincide with the height of good fishing. If that is the case, I would contact your prospective guide, and see what they recommend both in terms of species and methods. After all, they are the expert, and you should consider what they recommend. No guide wants to take you out on a bad fishing trip, and the best ones care just as much or more than you do about the success of your trip. They will not recommend that you go after something that is not biting well, and soliciting their advice on what to do often leads to some very cool experiences you would have missed otherwise.

However, do not automatically do whatever they suggest, and make sure your own priorities are being met as well. Sometimes doing exactly what you want will not be productive and compromise will have to be made, but figure out what compromises you are willing to make and which you are not. For instance, if you arrive in August and you want to fly fish for stripers and your prospective captain suggests trolling for bluefish and then some bottom fishing, that is probably not a trip that is going to make you happy, no matter how good trolling for bluefish and bottom fishing may be at the time. It will probably be possible to catch stripers, but wire-line will probably be a more effective choice than a fly rod. It is likely that you will be able to catch fish on the fly, but they will be bluefish. Determine whether you prefer to change your species or methods, sacrificing both will probably not be necessary. If a main reason you wanted striped bass was for table fare, but you have a better shot at the equally delicious fluke or sea bass, are you open to that? Do you want a lot of action no matter where it comes from, or are species and methods more of a priority than a constant bent rod? Talk about these options with your prospective captain, and consider their suggestions and be flexible, yet make sure in the end you get to do what you want to do. If a particular captain seems too set on one course of action, try talking to other captains, but if most seem hesitant or unwilling to do something, it is probably for a good reason. By the same token, beware of a captain who makes promises that sound too good to be true. Again using the hypothetical August striper fly fishing trip as an example, while a hot striper bite accessible on fly is not impossible at that time, it is unlikely, and most captains will tell you that. If you talk to a few captains who do not foresee it being productive, and then you find one who is happy to give it a shot and seems optimistic about your chances it would certainly not be the first time one captain has enjoyed success while others scratched their heads, but be sure to inquire further. Why is he optimistic when everybody else is not? Is he fishing different places, different tides, will you be fishing at night rather than during the day? If they are hesitant to provide answers or corroboration of good fishing, consider the possibility that it is because they are short on answers themselves and are perhaps a little unscrupulous in their claims.

Just like any other profession, there are professional fishermen who are very, very good at what they do, there are guys who get the job done, and there are some incompetents. Unfortunately, as the customer, you have the job of figuring out who is who, and that is not always easy to do. The guy who advertises the most may not be the best fisherman and the guy with the nicest boat may not be the best fisherman. In the world of charter fishing there are generally full-timers and part-timers. There are guys who try to make their living fishing and they are out with clients every day, all season, every chance they get. There are also guys who get their captains license and take a few trips here and there to pay for fuel and tackle and perhaps finance a portion of their own fishing. I have nothing against the part-timers and most of them are very fine fishermen, very capable teachers, and a pleasure to fish with. Someday I may even become one, but your odds of getting stuck with an incompetent certainly rise when you go with a guy who isn't doing it all the time, and if a guy can make it full time, it is probably at least partially due to competence.

Experience is an important factor to take into account, but consider there may be such a thing as too experienced. As a captain on the younger side, I may be biased, but consider that a captain with forty years experience has already seen more stripers than he ever thought he would, he has had so many happy clients and disappointed clients that he has been numbed to both, and he is very tired. You may want to consider somebody who is still young and excitable but who isn't necessarily figuring things out as he goes along.

When looking for a captain on Nantucket, you have a lot of options. You can share a boat with others for a reasonable per-person rate, or you can charter the whole boat and fish by yourself or take only your chosen guests. If budgetary concerns are paramount, and you only want to bend a rod, going on a head boat (pay by the person) may be the answer, but keep in mind, under those circumstances it is not what you want to do, but what a group wants to do, and usually that means what the captain wants to do. Be sure to speak with the captain about what types of fishing he plans to do and what he plans to fish for. This usually entails trolling for bluefish, or maybe stripers in the harbor, and perhaps bottom fishing.

Coast Guard regulations make the limit for most charter boats six people, but some are licensed for more than six, and a few are limited to fewer due to size. If you are in a party of eight and you all want to be on the same boat, that quickly limits who you can fish with and what you can do.

Straight Wharf is the epicenter for charter fishing on Nantucket, and it is home to the head boats the *Herbert T* and the *Just Do It Too*. For a private charter, where you pay for the entire boat and fish only with your guests, there is Captain Josh Eldridge's *Monomoy* (which can take more than six people), Bob DeCosta's *Albacore*, Brain Borgeson's *Absolute*, and my boat, the *Topspin*. There are also several charter boats that operate out of Madaket and more on the town pier. Years ago it may have been more accurate to equate the Straight Wharf fleet with heavy tackle trolling and offshore fishing, whereas Madaket was home to the casting and fly-fishing crowd, but that is not really the case anymore. Heavy tackle trolling is sort of a last resort onboard *Topspin*, casting onboard the *Albacore* is common, and light-tackle pursuits onboard the *Monomoy* are also possible when appropriate. To further muddy the waters a few Madaket guys are venturing offshore these days. Flats fishing and bonito fishing are shorter run from Madaket, and I normally depart from there on all my flats and bonito trips, whereas town is more proximate to Great Point and the eastern shore.

Regardless of where you fish out of, communication with your captain is important both before and during the trip. If you would prefer to catch fish on spinning gear rather than trolling, if you want to try for stripers, but you would rather use live bait than troll wire line, if a delicious dinner is a priority and you want to definitely do some bottom fishing for fluke and sea bass, these are all things that are usually possible, but your captain needs to know about them ahead of time to be sure he is prepared and to be sure you have booked the boat for enough time. You do not want to arrive at your boat after having booked a two and half hour trip expecting a multi-species trip to Sankaty only to learn upon your arrival at the dock that the ride to Sankaty and back is an hour each way.

If you are a fly fisherman, it is important to discuss that as well. Will you be bringing your own fly rod, and if not, does your captain have one for you? Does he have flies or will you be expected to bring your own? I think in the early days of saltwater fly fishing it was much more common for anglers to have to provide their own fly gear, today most fly fishing guides are going to have the rod and flies, but these are important questions. Are you exclusively a fly fisherman, or do want a spinning rod onboard in case it is windy? Would you like to start out spinfishing until you get a fish or two and then try for one on the fly? There are some captains out there who advertise fly fishing and to them it means trolling with a fly rod, and some anglers out there who think this is just fine. Is that fine with you or do you want to actually fly fish?

While you should be honest with the captain about your fishing abilities all the time, it is particularly important if you are a fly fisherman. Every fly-fishing guide in the world has stories about people who claimed to be experienced and competent fly fishermen, only to have them struggle mightily getting the fly out of the boat. If you are a beginner, be honest. It is likely the guide will be able put you in some situations where long casts are not necessary. If you would like some pointers on casting, your guide will probably be happy to give them to you, but may not want to insult you by offering unwanted advice. Guides, myself included, are usually very happy to spend a portion of your fishing trip teaching you to throw a fly. It can be great if your priority is to learn how to fly fish, but if your priority is to catch fish, you should be comfortable with a fly rod before you get on the boat. Now, by no means am I suggesting you need to be an expert, and do not hesitate to fly fish regardless of your skill level if that is what you want to do. When you are with a guide, you are paying for his time. You could pay him for four hours and spend two of those hours learning and practicing how to throw a fly and two hours fishing, and this is a wonderful way to spend the morning and I recommend it highly if you have the time and money. But if you are short on one or the other or both, consider buying a Lefty Kreh DVD on casting for about $20, practice in your backyard on your own time, and spend then entire four hours with your guide fishing. You can learn to cast anywhere, you don't even need water, and that may be the thing to do in order to maximize your guided fly-fishing experience.

There is also the possibility of going out with a beach guide. Frankly, I would not recommend it unless catching fish from the beach is your priority. Going out in a boat is going to be much more consistently successful, though I could be somewhat jaded because I once went on a guided beach fishing trip that was a huge disaster, and a good cautionary tale. It was during one summer that I was working as a mate in Madaket for the retired gentlemen and our normal routine was to fish off the airport and hammer big bluefish, but by that time striper fishing was getting better every year, and we had managed to take a few already by throwing swimming plugs into the breakers and whitewater along the sides of the Madaket cut. In any case, my boss was being visited by a cousin who wanted to catch a striped bass and who expressed a desire to do so from the beach rather than a boat. My boss was a man of substantial means, and in an attempt to please his cousin, he hired a beach guide. There was an extra seat in the car, so I was invited along. At this point, I had a little bit of experience with stripers, but not much, and I was eager for more. I looked forward to the trip very much, excited to catch a striper and equally excited to learn a new spot or two. I knew a lot of striper action took place in the harbor, and I guessed that was where our guide would show us a striper hotspot or two. We met the guide, and he informed us that we would be headed to Great Point. Now, I do not mean to suggest that stripers are never caught at Great Point, and there are sections in this book describing striper fishing at Great Point, both from the beach and from a boat, but he took us straight to the Northwest side of the Point and advised us to cast a Ballistic Missile or a Hopkins. I had spent plenty of days throwing Ballistic Missiles and Hopkins off Great Point prior to that day, and I had never caught any stripers nor seen any stripers caught there. I knew we were not going to catch any stripers that day either, and the guide seemed to think that was alright. When asked about stripers, he remarked how he had seen one caught in June or he knew somebody who caught one in June, or some such nonsense. In any case, after spending a big chunk of the summer absolutely crushing big bluefish off the airport, my boss shelled out a few hundred bucks to be driven to Great Point with his cousin and me, where I ended up catching a few small blues once I walked away from the barren spot where he suggested we cast to a spot I knew usually held some fish. My boss and his cousin got blanked because they could not cast far enough.

Now, I am not sure who was responsible for that debacle, perhaps my boss was not clear about what he expected, perhaps the guide thought he was taking out a group of tourists who would be very happy to see the lighthouse and perhaps get a couple bluefish, or perhaps he was not honest with my boss, drastically exaggerating our chances at striped bass and his own knowledge of island fishing. I got the distinct sense that his "guide service" was more of a taxi ride to Great Point and rod rental, rather than being taken fishing by an expert with extensive knowledge of tactics and locations. In any case, it is a prime example of what can happen when there is a lack of communication between the captain or guide and the customer, and the importance of choosing a good guide.

However, if catching fish with your feet in the sand is a priority, there are several reputable and competent beach guides out there, just take care to communicate your expectations as well as listen to their suggestions for good fishing.

When I am traveling somewhere new and fishing with a guide, I will always try to do it at the beginning of my trip in order to try and pick up on some tactics and possible locations that I can use while I am fishing on my own the rest of the trip. I recommend that you are up front about this with your captain or guide and in my experience, a good guide is happy to help. Certainly when my customers express a desire to fish on their own I try to advise them as best as I can. Most captains and guides are also happy to act as teachers, and when they know that you want to try and have some success on your own will they often slow down and explain how and why they are doing certain things, rather than just doing them quickly in order to get you onto the fish. They will often clue you in to critical subtleties about the spot, the tackle, the fish or the methods that would have gone unnoticed, and they usually have a pretty good supply of current fishing information. If you are going striper fishing with a guide, but you hope to find some blues later on your own, he will probably know where they have been, and may even show you if it is convenient. The idea the captain or guide might not show you his best spots or tactics if he thinks you are going to replicate them should not be much of a concern. A good captain or guide thrives on repeat customers and reputation, and by giving you good advice and showing you good fishing, he will probably get you to fish with him again, perhaps even more so if you do find some success on your own, and you will be likely to say good things about him and recommend him to others.

When choosing somebody to take you fishing, plan ahead, do some homework, ask some questions, and make sure you and your captain or guide are on the same page as far as species and tactics, as well as what your priorities are if things do not fall into place perfectly and plans need to be altered to salvage the day.

LAST CAST

Good fishing and the health of our oceans is not something to take for granted. When fishing, try to embrace sound conservation practices. If you are not going to eat what you catch, release it quickly and carefully. Use circle and single hooks whenever possible, especially if you plan to release your fish. Be cognizant of the ecosystem as a whole and treat the beaches and ocean with respect. Doing your part goes a long way.

You may want to join the fight ensure good fishing for years and generations to come. It is my hope that this book is optimistic and non-controversial whereas fisheries management, on every level from state to international, is generally heated and depressing. Therefore, I will not go into specifics, but there are many organizations out there, both large and small, dedicated to conserving our marine resources, as well as the public's right to fish, and they can use all the support they can get.

Nantucket is a wonderful place to fish. The fishing is excellent, and the crowds and competition are a fraction of what you can expect at many mainland fishing hotspots. Whether you are looking to bend a rod on some bluefish, fish bait on the bottom for dinner, head offshore for tuna, or stalk stripers on the flats with a fly rod, Nantucket offers something for everyone.

There are many places, many methods, many lures and many times to catch fish around Nantucket. While it has been my intent to write a broad and inclusive guide, there are certainly more options available to island anglers than those found within these pages. Do not hesitate to try a spot or a method just because it was not touched upon here. An important piece of fishing advice to keep in mind is that you are most assuredly not going to catch anything sitting on the couch.

In order to wrap things up, I leave you with my ideal fishing calendar. Keep in mind that it will change depending on the weather and numerous other factors from year to year, but it may serve as a quick reference for what is normally happening at any given time.

April

- Get all fishing gear out, organized and ready to go
- Depending on fishing reports from Martha's Vineyard, maybe hit the South Shore in search of schoolies

May

- Start off the month fishing the South Shore for schoolies
- Try to find the first keeper, perhaps along the South Shore, Great Point or in Nantucket Harbor
- Fish Nantucket Harbor by boat and beach, particularly creeks mouths on falling tides
- Look for the first bluefish off Dionis or Coatue, preferably high tide
- Black Sea Bass on the wreck
- End the month on the flats of Madaket

June

- Stripers everywhere
- Fish the Madaket and Tuckernuck flats as much as possible
- For fast action in a big boat, fish the Old Man
- Bluefin may start to make appearances offshore
- Look for stripers in the edge at Great Point as the month draws to a close

July

- When the east tide coincides with dawn, get the fly rods and light spinners and head to Great Point for striper action on the edge.
- If bluefishing in the outer rips, be prepared to release plenty of large striped bass
- Fishing Sankaty should yield mixed bag and lots of action
- Do not overlook bluefish for some fun in the sun
- Keep an ear out for reports of offshore action, both to the south and east

August

- Bonito arrive- fish Bonito Bar as much as possible
- Head south for dolphin, tuna, and hopefully marlin
- East for bluefin may be excellent as well
- Perhaps False Albacore arrive at the end of the month

September

- Keep fishing the Bonito Bar but keep in mind bonito and false albacore could pop up anywhere
- Great Point may offer good multispecies days
- Re-examine the flats for stripers
- The Old Man and Quidnet Rip may heat up
- An evening trip to the South Shore to cast a plug is not a bad idea
- Productive trips east for bluefin remain a strong possibility

October

- Get in a few last trips before a long winter
- Striped bass, bluefish, false albacore and bluefin remain possibilities

November

- Rumored to have good striper fishing years ago
- Over the last several years, giant bluefin bites have often occurred in November, but weather and conditions are a concern

December-March

- Head south as much as possible to become the visitor instead of the local, and the customer instead of the guide. Here are a few trips and guides that I personally recommend:
- Fish Southwest Florida with Capt. Matt Mitchell: http://www.capt-mattmitchell.com/
- Fish the Florida Keys and Miami with Capt. Rich Smith: http:// www.captainrichsmith.com/
- Fish Costa Rica with Capt. John Brennan: http://www.captainjohn-brennan.com/

I love fishing and I love Nantucket. I have often said that if you need to be catching fish to have fun fishing, you should find another sport. The more existential successes of fishing, such as time spent in nature and the pursuit of the illusive, are perhaps more important than caught fish. While I have said it, and I believe it, I certainly have trouble living it at times. Having fun catching fish is much easier than having to search for imperceptible victories. I hope this book helps you catch a few more fish, and if it somehow helps with the bigger picture, that is great too. Good luck, and I will see you on the water.

ABOUT THE AUTHOR

Matt Reinemo is a Nantucket native. He grew up fishing the ponds and beaches with his mother, and chasing bluefish with his father, becoming a total fishing nut by high school. He earned his captain's license when he turned eighteen and is now in his fourteenth season as a full-time captain and guide.

Higher education led Matt south toward more fish (not coincidently) where he graduated from Drew University and the University of Miami School of Law. After a very short time in an office, the appeal of the ocean proved too great, and Matt returned to fishing. In the winter, he has scalloped, travelled, and run sportfishing boats in Costa Rica and Florida. His fishing column, "Recently Hooked," appeared in the Nantucket *Independent*. When Matt is not guiding clients, he enjoys cooking, reading, and racquet sports, but still prefers to be fishing.

He lives on Nantucket with his wife, who is becoming a skilled angler out of necessity. He looks forward to fishing with his son, who is now one. This is Matt's first book.

To fish with Captain Matt, email him at mattreinemo@gmail.com or visit:
www.facebook.com/FishingNantucket
www.fishingnantucket.com

Made in the USA
Charleston, SC
30 June 2012